REFLECT

THE ART <u>OF</u> POWERFUL
SALES COMMUNICATION

REFLECT

THE ART OF POWERFUL SALES COMMUNICATION

BY MATT DETJEN

Foreword by Jane Allen,
Smart Work | Network founder

SPO!LER ALERT
PUBLISHING
Simpsonville, SC

REFLECT: The Art of Powerful Sales Communication
Matthew E. Detjen

 SPO!LER ALERT
PUBLISHING

Spoiler Alert Publishing
www.spoileralertpublishing.com
Simpsonville, SC

Paperback ISBN: 979-8-9911124-0-6
E-book ISBN: 979-8-9911124-1-3
Library of Congress Control Number: 2024914181

Edited by Cindy Dashnaw Jackson, Cause Communications
Cover designed by Jenni Roberts, ARC Studios
Typesetting by Journey Bound Publishing
First Printing
Printed in the United States of America

Disclaimer

The following work reflects the thoughts and views of the author only; they do not reflect those of his past employers, present employer, or future employers.

Jane Allen has granted the author permission to write his interpretation of her training course, *Powerful Sales Communication* (PSC). With permission, the author utilized course-specific materials (participant manuals and facilitator guides).

This work is intended to be informative and educational. The author provides the information herein with the understanding that he is not rendering legal, accounting, or other professional services.

All trademarks referenced in this book are the property of their respective owners, and no authors were directly quoted by the author.

In the spirit of *education* and *fair use*, the author approves brief quotations of his work without permission.

Dedicated to

Vito Giordano (1934 – 2020)
Captain, US Navy; Fordham University

Scott Crandall (1949 – 2022)
Commissioned Officer, Military Intelligence,
US Army; United States Military Academy
at West Point

and to

My wife, Joellyn,
who has been my forever cheerleader
and continues to ride shotgun on every
new adventure.

To my children, Elle and Heidi;
as I view the future through your eyes, you
remind me that we should never stop dreaming.

And to my parents, Harold and Nancy Detjen,
who showed me what hard work looked like and
never dismissed a single one of my dreams.

Contents

REFLECT

Foreword By Jane Allen
Founder, Smart Work | Network

In the early 2000s, my training and development firm seized a valuable opportunity to deliver a sales training course to sales representatives at one of the world's largest and most well-respected tire manufacturers. Our course, *Powerful Sales Communication* (PSC), had just undergone a significant transformation, embracing a more experiential and immersive learning approach. The inaugural session of our revamped course was in beautiful San Francisco, a place I love to visit, so I attended the class with a keen eye to evaluate the course's effectiveness.

That was when I met Matt Detjen.

The course kicked off with videoed attendee role-plays designed to assess each participant's baseline skills in active listening and sales communication. Matt immediately distinguished himself during his initial role-play, show-casing an impressive level of competence for someone still relatively young in his career (he was 31 at the time). During a break on the second day, Matt approached me with an enthusiasm for the course that practically radiated from his pores. He inquired about my involvement in the program, and I couldn't help but commend his exceptional role-plays and ask where he had acquired such remarkable skills. Matt humbly mentioned his experience in nonprofit fundraising, completion of an intensive Dale Carnegie sales training program post-bachelor's degree, and time working as a commercial model and actor.

Recognizing his exceptional potential, I agreed to exchange contact information and encouraged him to stay in touch, even suggesting he might one day teach the course himself.

As steadfast believers in the law of attraction (promoted by thought leaders like Napoleon Hill) and the concept of flow (attributed to psychologist Mihaly Csikszentmihalyi), neither Matt nor I are surprised that we have stayed connected for almost two decades. Matt's belief in *Powerful Sales Communication* would only grow over the years, eventually culminating in him recommending my firm and this training to two of his employers. What's more, he went on to become a certified co-facilitator alongside my firm's lead facilitator. Interestingly, one of the companies he recommended us to while he led their sales training efforts was acquired by the same company where our paths first crossed. Matt now leads the North American sales training efforts in his original organization. Life sure has a way of coming full circle!

In 2021, 14 years after our initial meeting, Matt reached out with a unique request. He asked for my permission to write a book about *Powerful Sales Communication*. I was genuinely delighted he wanted to take on this endeavor. My only request was that he dedicate the book to two remarkable individuals—people who Matt, in his nod to George Lucas' *Star Wars* film franchise, fondly refers to as "Jedi Master" communications trainers—who were instrumental in imparting these skills to him: Vito Giordano and Scott Crandall.

Vito Giordano, our first master communications trainer, served as my senior facilitator for *Powerful Sales Communication* for over a decade. His ability to convey the course's content and offer precise, humorous feedback endeared him to countless participants. Vito passed away in 2020 and leaves a legacy of thousands trained in these vital skills.

Another key figure in my journey with Matt, the second "Jedi Master," was Scott Crandall. In the early 2000s, Scott led North American sales training at Matt's employer, the same global tire manufacturer I first mentioned. Scott recognized the potency of *Powerful Sales Communication* and gave the green light to what would become 10 years of training their sales professionals. Under Vito's tutelage, Scott mastered the art of facilitating the course and took on the role of lead instructor once Vito retired. During this transition, Matt proved himself a capable co-facilitator, demonstrating he had truly mastered the skills and was ready to pass them on to others. Scott passed away in early 2022. In the truest form of attraction and flow, Matt now holds the same position Scott held when he first contracted with my firm to deliver *Powerful Sales Communication*. Wow! Today, Matt has ascended to the role of master communications trainer of *Powerful Sales Communication* skills. I invite you to read this book, which aptly captures the essence of his mastery—a reflection of his ability to listen attentively and understand customer concerns before presenting his own perspective. I commend Matt for his exceptional mastery of these skills, his ability to distill them into a concise and accessible book, and for generously sharing personal examples that facilitate practical learning. *REFLECT* offers insights that transcend sales and move into the realm of active listening, a fundamental aspect of all meaningful communication.

The book is also an eloquent tribute to Vito and Scott, two true training masters and cherished friends who profoundly influenced this journey. As I contemplate my own legacy, I take immense pride in passing on the work we initiated to adept facilitators like Matt—successful individuals who have the ability to impart these invaluable skills to their own circles of influence and beyond.

Conversations where both parties listen with the intent to understand each other are the foundation of any sincere relationship. In sales, these types of conversations are essential for building trust, uncovering needs, and turning prospects into loyal customers. *REFLECT* is a primer for helping you build these trust-filled business relationships, ***one conversation at a time!***

– *Jane*

REFLECT

Introduction

A brag on Jane

I attended PSC in the first years that Jane's company, Smart Work | Network, offered it. Jane would have a continuous, decade-long run at selling this course to my then-employer. In my 25+ year career, I have had the great fortune of working for and interacting with companies who consistently invest in training, and I can tell you that the popularity and staying power of PSC I've witnessed is a testament to the material. It is truly rare that an outside training course, taught by an outside vendor, is retained by a large corporation, like the one I worked for all those years ago (and do again today), for such a duration. Bravo, Jane!

Like many businesses, Jane's morphed with time. Her passion for predictive assessments, talent consulting, and executive search would finally see PSC put gently on a shelf (like a prized trophy) after a phenomenal run. Jane and I would talk for years about the next chapter for PSC, but pulling it down from its place of honor simply to start teaching it again never felt grand enough. It deserved something bigger. Giving every salesperson access to the material via this book feels right!

This book is a deep dive into everything that makes the material forever relevant for any salesperson aspiring to have an edge over their competition. Jane, thank you for the trust and permission to tell the PSC story and for your words of wisdom sprinkled throughout these pages. For you, the reader ... get ready! It's time to step into the classroom with me!

1

A Sales Wakeup Call
It's not them, it's us

"I don't listen to you," I said to my wife.

We were sharing a Friday night drink in the kitchen and reflecting on the week, as we often did (and still do). This particular conversation was 17 years ago, but the memory is still vivid. "Of course, you do! You're a great listener," said Jo (short for Joellyn), offering support while subtly implying I was being ridiculous. Knowing me as she does, she might also have been bracing herself for one of my dry, often bad jokes.

I assured her I was serious.

The year was 2007. We were brand-new Sacramento residents, recently relocated from Indiana. I was a senior account manager at a global tire manufacturer, engaging in B2B (business-to-business) outside sales in roughly two-thirds of the state. My career was taking off, and Jo was working locally in brand marketing. Both still young in our work and marriage, we saw California as an exciting time and place in our personal and professional lives.

Jo was fresh off her commute that evening, and I had just returned home from a multi-day sales training course in San Francisco sponsored by my employer. When I signed up for the course, *Powerful Sales Communication* (PSC), I had no idea it would forever change the way I looked at my own communication skills in every part of my life. I had no idea I would meet Jane Allen, the brains and heart behind PSC—a woman who would become a mentor and lifelong friend. I had no clue I would one day facilitate the course with the man who instructed me (for all you *Star Wars* fans, meeting him was truly a Jedi/Padawan moment). And I certainly never dreamed I would be so moved by the principles and concepts that, after years of personal application, I would put pen to paper and write this book.

My wife was kind enough to refute my proclamation of subpar listening skills that evening but, unbeknownst to us, we both still had an inferior definition of the word "listening" back then (at least I sure did). I know now that it's one thing to *hear* someone's words, but something else entirely to take them in, quickly sort them out in your head, and toss a piece of understanding back at the speaker without judgment or a solution in order to (1) check your understanding as their story progresses and (2) give the speaker a green light and ample runway to continue.

Spoiler alert: *I just profiled reflecting, the key to your future sales success.*

I said to Jo, "Sure, I always hear the words you say, but I rarely (I gave myself a little credit) demonstrate understanding." This epiphany had arrived during my drive home, since the slow speed at which rush-hour traffic from San Francisco to Sacramento moves (insert yawn here) is great for deep thinking and personal reflection. A lot of personal reflection, in fact. On this particular snail's-pace drive, I was in full self-diagnosis mode, replaying and judging countless personal and business conversations against the last two-and-a-half days of lessons in PSC.

As I drove home, it hit me that I rarely listen to gain a clear understanding, let alone simply let the speaker empty their emotional and/or detail-filled bucket. (Remember this "bucket" concept; you'll see it again). I usually wanted the most basic facts presented quickly so I could solve what I perceive to be their problem or simply tell my similar story. As a newlywed, for instance, I would take in the surface-level bullet points of my wife's problems and then go for a *Wheel of Fortune* moment: "I'd like to solve the puzzle!" Think about family and friends excited to talk about a recent vacation. Many of us are quick to stop these poor souls after only a few sentences to tell them about our own trips. "Wait, you went to Miami? We went to Miami, too!"

Don't get me wrong; wanting to share is human, and longing to help someone fix a problem is a noble pursuit.

Assuming that's what they want at any given moment is where we go astray.

Spoiler alert: *Sometimes we just need to let something pour out of us and into someone else's ear without our listener solving anything.*

This behavior should not come as a shocker, as we've all done it with friends and loved ones—but what may stop you in your tracks is the knowledge that many of us are the same way in business. It might be a hard pill to swallow, but the scenarios above do not constitute listening in our business interactions, either. If we are honest with ourselves, we can all think of a time when a customer told us, either verbally or with their body language, that we were not hearing them. A memory might even be hitting you right now—your own Sacramento kitchen moment, your "I don't listen to you" moment.

Take a second if you need one, because this can be a shot to the ol' ego. I know it was for me.

Something had clicked for me that day: My relentless efforts to resolve issues and tell my "one up" stories were 100-percent counterproductive. I was unthinkingly shutting down conversations in my personal and professional interactions. I was flashing a red light and robbing speakers of their runway.

I was unwittingly prolonging or even sabotaging my sales journeys with customers.

Right now, you might be admitting, "Guilty! So now what? Therapy, quit sales, run away with the circus?" None of the above—just keep reading and be willing to jump into the PSC lessons I learned with me. The principles taught in PSC significantly improved my professional interactions and, if you cannot already tell, had an equally positive impact on my personal life. (I'm still married!) It was the communication wake-up call I needed and I bet you need, too.

Three main sales-related PSC themes have materialized for me over the years. Here they are in order (because the order matters):

1. We all want to feel *heard*, and your customers are no different. Engaging in genuine listening, also known as active or reflective listening, will ensure that anyone speaking to you will feel heard.

2. Going on a shared, authentic journey with a customer is a direct result of the questions you ask and the reciprocal active/reflective listening you engage in. This productive journey is the prize for great listening because the needs you'll uncover will be real for the customer and for you.

3. Persuasion is not a bad word, and you will have earned the right to be persuasive at the end of a shared, authentic journey of discovery. You will have built real rapport with your customer and identified real needs (not your preconceived notions), so they're ready to be sold and probably even rooting for you by now.

Spoiler alert: *The PSC skills you learn here will dramatically change the way you sell. If you apply them correctly and consistently, they will at a minimum change the way you listen and thus improve your personal life.*

By now, you're justifiably asking, "Who is this guy?" I get it; I also size up speakers and so-called experts. Here are some of my milestones and accomplishments after learning PSC skills:

- In the first year after I finished PSC, I won the top North American B2B sales award, *Pacesetter*, which ranked me in the **top 2 percent of all B2B salespeople** working for a global tire manufacturer.
- I won **Rookie of the Year** while selling for the largest group purchasing organization (GPO) operating in the North American commercial transportation sector.
- I wrote a **sales process** for a global off-road mobility solution provider that would be adopted across and beyond North America.
- I taught PSC principles to **globally recognized brands** from Jane Allen's client list.
- I took the leadership helm of my employer's **North American region B2B sales training team** in 2023, the team responsible for training our own and customers' employees.
- I have made some **astounding sales**. One in particular I'll share in later chapters.

My inspiration for writing this book was rooted in *a need to demystify sales success*. Salespeople and sales leaders alike think the next great sales process will be the secret sauce for a record year. While a sales process is absolutely necessary, it's just half of the equation. It's what we do *within* a sales process that becomes the game-changer.

Here's where PSC stands alone among sales training programs. It's not a sales process, *per se*. **PSC is a communication methodology that will breathe life into any**

sales process and yield unmatched results when correctly applied.

Jane calls PSC "the heart of selling." Your sales game could simply be missing some heart. Let's find it.

2

A [Powerful] Sales Relationship Process
Your sales process is (probably) fine

Search the internet for "sales process." Go ahead, I'll wait.

Now, if you click on the *IMAGES* tab of your search results page, you will be bombarded with diagrams of every hue, usually comprising floating balls (for some reason) and arrows, with stages or phases resembling this:

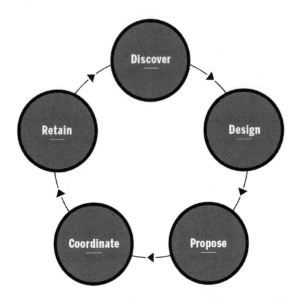

True story, right? Is it hitting you? *They are all fundamentally the same!* Seriously. And that's not a bad thing; it means that nearly everyone following a sales process is using the correct roadmap. We're all on the right track for relationship sales. No therapy needed!

A NOTE ON RELATIONSHIP VS. COMPETITIVE SALES

This book focuses on *relationship* sales—typically a business-to-business (B2B) sale where the products and/or services are solving a problem or improving a process for the customer. One lap around this kind of sales process/cycle takes enough time and effort to form a *relationship*, hence the name.

Competitive sales, the other side of the coin, can be done in days, hours, even minutes. Think quick business-to-consumer (B2C) sales. Though this book doesn't focus on competitive sales, the skills taught here will help you, too, see a higher close rate.

THE FAMILIAR SALES PROCESS

PSC doesn't reinvent the sales process:

1. In **Prequalification** (not included in the illustration above), a salesperson attempts to find out everything they can about a prospect before making contact. You're scratching just below the surface with facts you can easily mine to make an informed decision whether to pursue or abandon.

2. **Discover**, better known as the *discovery phase*, is typically the longest part of any sales process. Your needs assessment happens in this phase; you're probing, looking, and listening for a legitimate need or a place to partner.

3. **Design** is where you create a money-saving or revenue-generating offer (your actual proposal).

4. **Propose** is your ask. Your moment of glory!

5. **Coordinate** comes into play after you make the sale. You did it! Once you're done slapping high-fives like Maverick and Goose in *Top Gun*, it's time to assemble your team, put the pieces in place for success, and focus on retaining your customer (the next step).

6. **Retain** means you set key performance indicators (KPIs) and regularly report them to the customer. You're getting sticky with the customer, doing the things that will enhance your relationship. We answer the one question (among others) that really matters: Did you and your product/service do what you

promised? Answering this question, even informally, is at the heart of customer retention and a key to keeping your competition away.

If you noticed (shout-out to all detail-oriented readers who did), an arrow in the sales process illustration now points you back to **Discover,** denoting a cycle. Why? Most salespeople want continued and new sales with existing customers, right? A great sales process follows a certain order (process) and repeats itself (cycle) by design. When we find ourselves in the **Retain** (retention) phase, we should already be focused on the customer's next problem to keep them coming back for more.

If we take our roadmap analogy to the extreme, it actually has us driving in a perpetual circle. You're in a roundabout, but you're not exiting on purpose. Exiting would mean you gave up or got the boot!

That's it—less than three minutes to describe a universal sales process for relationship sales. Much of it probably wasn't a surprise. Your sales process—any sales process, as we've seen—is simply there to keep you on track.

And we don't need to rewrite or replace your sales process, as you ideally have one tailored to your business. We just need to learn how to apply it correctly. (If you don't have a sales process, please steal the one above.)

TAKING OUR SALES PROCESS ON THE ROAD

Now that we've got our process, our sales roadmap, if you will, what about the destination? On the PSC map, all roads—Prequalifying Avenue, Discover Street, Design Route, Propose Lane—lead to the sale.

I hear you: "Really? But, Matt, every sale is different." You are correct; your (prospective) customer's needs are ever-changing. *Even so, the sales process remains the same.* The steps never change, and the finish line is always the sale. (See, we don't need to ever reinvent or buy a new process.)

The needs of even the most similar customers will diverge, I promise you. Sure, both FedEx and UPS are worldwide logistics experts with trucks, planes, forklifts, hubs, and people, but I will bet the farm that what's keeping the good people of FedEx up at night isn't even on the UPS radar screens, and vice versa. They have different needs, but they don't require different sales processes.

It's OK to assume similarities exist, of course—when you know a great deal about Company A, it's a no-brainer to apply some of the lessons learned to Company B. However, a major mistake we make as salespeople is to assume similar companies can't possibly have *dissimilar* needs. The lesson here: Always assuming carbon-copy needs for similar companies will leave you in the middle of the salesperson pack, if not bringing up the rear. Your customer can smell a presumptive salesperson from a mile away. Be real with yourself and catch your assumptions before your customers do.

PSC: A [POWERFUL] SALES RELATIONSHIP PROCESS

We've established that each customer has their own needs. Now we can look at finding and addressing those needs within the framework of PSC … a [powerful] sales relationship process designed to set you apart from your competition!

The best part? PSC, if applied correctly, lives primarily within the **Discovery**, **Design,** and **Propose** stages of your greater sales process. Think of PSC as a process within a process.

With a through-theme of listening and reflecting, PSC has four stages:

1. Build rapport.
2. Understand needs.
3. Deliver solutions.
4. Close the interaction.

If you are rolling your eyes at the seeming simplicity of these four steps, don't close the book just yet. I promised this material changed my life, significantly improving the way I conducted sales and my personal interactions with family and friends. (Heck, it made my interactions with strangers more productive!) I stand by that promise. At this moment, I hope I'm already making you think about how PSC might plug into the sales strategies you already know and love, how it might marry with your company's sales process, and what the magic is behind this powerful approach.

We're getting ready to dig deep into the skills needed to perfect each stage. I aim to reveal what the award-winning salespeople are doing ... the President's Club members, the Pacesetters, the money-makers. My goal is to demystify the blueprint for sales success, and let me assure you, I will challenge you along the way. If nothing else, I will make you a better listener ... the heart of sales success demystification.

We're now on the same page with a sales process and the stages we'll focus on through the PSC lens. The next chapters will show you how to boost your communication skills into the stratosphere … and watch your sales results follow. Let's go!

Spoiler alert: *Self-critiquing your listening skills may be painful. We can get through it. I'll be your guide, cheerleader, and maybe even therapist along the way.*

REFLECT

3

Building Real Rapport
Skip the fish

"Would you look at that whopper!" The visiting salesperson gestures to the customer's 23-inch rainbow trout mounted on the wall.

"Somebody's an athlete!" The salesperson nods and smiles at the framed marathon finish-line photo on the customer's desk.

"How about those (insert the area's sports team)!" The salesperson strides through the warehouse to fist bump the customer's hand, trying to seem familiar with the local sports scene.

Face it, we've all made this kind of ridiculously obvious small talk with customers to break the ice and build an instant connection. Many salespeople think this works. *It does not.* At best, it creates a temporary, surface-level connection; at worst, it can doom your credibility from the get-go with the wrong individual.

Building genuine rapport is the first stage in PSC. Calling rapport-building a stage is almost misleading, since you're building rapport throughout every step of the process. I call attention to it first for two reasons: (1) its sheer importance, and (2) because many people falsely try to build rapport only initially, then check it off their list.

Walk with me on a quick journey to witness the opposite of real rapport-building. A salesperson has an appointment with you. You welcome them into your office, where you happen to display some of your most prized possessions: rare baseball cards that you have been collecting since your childhood. The salesperson formally introduces themselves and the company they represent. They instantly notice your baseball card collection on the wall behind you, and with hardly a pause, questions bombard you as if from a Gatling gun: "Wow, how long have you been collecting cards? Is it an expensive hobby? Where in the world did you find all these? I bet collecting keeps you busy. Do you have Ozzie Smith's 1979 rookie card? Is that it?!? Can I touch it?"

Let's be real, that got kind of weird, especially at the end. The sad part is, something of this nature has happened to all of us when interacting with salespeople. And (therapy alert), if you're being honest with yourself as it relates to your chosen profession of sales, maybe you're having a "yes, guilty as charged" moment. But if this approach is so common, why is it wrong?

Let's break it down.

The salesperson told you their name, tossed in the company's name for good measure, peered around for the first thing they could see to get you talking ... and boom, they think they're building rapport. That's not real rapport-building. That, my friends, is what I call *the fish*. They chose a cheap, surface-level way to connect—in this case, baseball cards instead of a mounted trout—over the techniques that build real rapport in sales. (You could almost hear, "Would you look at that whopper!" couldn't you?) *The fish* is nothing more than an icebreaker, inconsequential small talk (with emphasis on "inconsequential"). It's irrelevant, illogical, trifling.

Disclaimer: These ice breakers, in very small doses, do have their place; I don't want you to think I'm some kind of anti-small-talk monster. If taken to the extreme, however, they open you up to sales derailment in two major ways: (1) they eat up way too much precious face time that could be used for needs discovery, and (2) they communicate you have nothing of substance to share.

I look at it like this: We all have a bullsh*t cap or threshold—an amount of time we permit small talk in a professional setting before getting down to business. You aren't conscious of your limit, but your brain tracks the time for you. Reflect on your own conversations where you were the buyer, and I bet you will find your bullsh*t threshold is about the same every time.

I have a new job for you: Your job is to pay attention to your customer's body language and verbal cues so you know when to start talking business. When customer-facing, it's about *their* bullsh*t threshold, not your need to get comfortable. I've heard too many customers prompt too many salespeople to "get on with it." Ouch! If they prompt you like this to get going, you definitely took it too far. My own bullsh*t threshold as a salesperson maxes out at less than two minutes; I'd better be building real rapport with my customer by then. (My threshold for *receiving* bullsh*t as a customer is the same. And I use such an unequivocal word as bullsh*t because that's what I think of non-rapport-building small talk.)

We will define what sales rapport-building looks, feels, and sounds like, but let's start with PSC's definition of **relationship selling**:

Relationship selling is a process where the customer and relationship manager (salesperson) build a long-term relationship while developing solutions together to meet specific customer needs. This relationship/connection includes:

1. the customer's general respect for and trust in the relationship manager, and
2. mutual understanding and agreement on what's important to the customer (the needs).

Let me draw your attention to "respect for and trust in the relationship manager." In our example above, did the salesperson earn your trust, or did they instead give you that crowded-elevator, you're-in-my-personal-space feeling? I'm betting that when they get around to telling you why they're there, you'd be tuned out. Why? Simple—they bypassed anything that might establish mutual respect, and in doing so, *they bypassed a foundation of real rapport-building*. Moral of the story: No matter the scenario, *the fish* is *the fish*.

No more about *the fish*—for now. But we'll be casting back to it later. (See what I did there? I warned you ... we're already wading into dad joke waters!)

REAL RAPPORT FOR STELLAR SALES: WHAT IS IT?

Two synonyms for rapport are *relationship* and *understanding*. We intentionally used both of those words in our definition of relationship selling (above) because to build rapport is to establish mutual respect, trust, and credibility. To quote Jane in the PSC Participant Guide:

> *Building trust and credibility, and ultimately rapport, involves creating an environment in which the customer feels there is little to no risk in doing business with you or your company. You create a customer-focused atmosphere of convenience and timeliness, and one that is solution-oriented. Your style sets the prospect or customer at ease. You exhibit a genuine understanding of the customer's [buying] style(s) and a willingness to modify your behavior to make them feel comfortable.*

I want to do business with a salesperson like the one Jane describes, don't you?

A well-known African proverb tells you how to eat an elephant: One bite at a time, of course! And that's how PSC approaches learning. Here's a bite on how to establish and build rapport.

- Be prepared and organized
- Adjust to your customer's learning style(s)
- Match body language/energy
- Appear confident
- Focus on the other person
- Listen and reflect

Let's dig into each of these principles individually, and maybe take another cast at the fish.

THE PSC PRINCIPLES FOR BUILDING RAPPORT IN SELLING

1. Be prepared and organized

Your preparation reveals volumes about you. Here are just a few examples of what being prepared and organized look like and why it matters:

- **You are specific and intentional about making appointments.** Don't be mysterious; professionals need a compelling reason to make time for you. Think about it: You are more likely to speak with a stranger who quickly identifies why they are approaching you than to one who pulls *the fish* on you, right? Briefly share what you want to discuss and why. Practice a quick introduction/elevator speech that isn't cheesy or pushy.
- **You are punctual.** Arrive 15 minutes early for in-person appointments. Use the time getting there (flight, drive, etc.) to collect your thoughts. Then enter the building: 15 minutes early is perfect, 10 minutes is

acceptable, on time is late. For virtual meetings, sign on 5 minutes early; be waiting for them.

- **You show up with a plan.** Showing up with a plan is a continuation of being specific about why you wanted the appointment in the first place. Vito Giordano, the master instructor who taught PSC for years, often reflected on a common simple formula for sharing information:

  (1) tell them what you are going to tell them (or what you want to accomplish),

  (2) tell them (do the thing you said you wanted to do), and

  (3) tell them what you told them (recap).

Telling your prospect what you are going to tell them is the foundation of a prepared and organized sales presentation. In the first few minutes of an interaction, every buyer tries to size up what's in it for them. No matter how informal the setting, lay out an agenda and check for any time constraints ("Do we still have 30 minutes?")

Spoiler alert: The customer might throw your plan out the window by leading the discussion down another road, especially during discovery sessions, and that's OK—you'll just have to call an audible. (For non-sports fans, this means to change your plan at the last minute because of unforeseen obstacles.) If you love the detour they're taking, then go with it. If you don't, referencing your plan might help pull the conversation back onto its original path. If they hand the discovery steering wheel back to you, grab it!

Your first interactions with your customer are hugely influential; they set the rapport-building wheels in motion. Be specific and intentional, be early, and show up with a plan.

2. Adjust to your customer's learning style(s)

This principle is not new to most seasoned salespeople, at least in theory. Consistently *applying* it and ultimately *mastering* it will give you a real edge over your competition.

Educators generally recognize four primary styles of learning: visual, auditory, kinesthetic, and reading/writing (Fleming and Mills, 1992). You (yes, this includes you) and your customers all respond to a combination of these four, relying more on some than others. While you will be unable to pinpoint the exact percentages of an individual customer's styles, you can learn the detectable cues that point you toward their *dominant* learning styles.

Learning style: Visual
These customers want to see it! Listen for comments such as:

- "I'd like to see that in action."
- "Can I see some examples of your work?"
- "Let me show you my issue."

Learning style: Auditory
These customers want to hear about it. They'll say things like:

- "I'd like to hear about your offer."
- "Tell me the highlights of the program."
- "Could you repeat that? I want to take it in one more time."

Learning style: Kinesthetic

These customers want to touch it. Listen for things like:

- "I'd like to operate that new [widget] myself."
- "I want to get a feel for how it handles."
- "Did you bring a sample I can hold?"

Learning style: Reading/Writing

These customers want to see it in print. They'll say:

- "Do you have a printed copy I can review?"
- "I need to put a calculator to what you're showing me."
- "Can you go back a page? I want to re-read that last paragraph."

Simple enough, yes? Four learning styles, easy to size up once we know how to listen. So, where do we typically go wrong? **Here's the answer:** *Most untrained salespeople unconsciously assume that every customer's combination of learning styles is exactly the same as their own.* They communicate with others as if they were selling to themselves. If you do this—STOP. To build rapport, you must listen for the cues and adjust your approach to match how the buyer is telling you they like to learn.

Spoiler alert: *This is next-level selling!* Rookies sell the way in which they like to learn themselves. Pros sell the way in which their customers like to learn. Full disclosure: I made the rookie mistake for years. You, too, can change!

3. Match body language/energy

Let's get *feng shui* for a moment: Matching your energy and body language to those of your customer can keep you in harmony, and harmony is important. Very important.

One of my learning styles is visual, so allow me to paint a picture. Think of your customer's body language as a roller-coaster ride. On any given roller coaster, the rider climbs peaks and descends into valleys and curves around turns. The ascents are slow, but the drops are fast; sometimes the ride's bumpy, other times the rider soars like a bird on the wing. In sales, the energy and body language of your customer is like riding the coaster, and your job is to hop right into the seat next to them and go along for the ride.

- If your customer is excited, then get excited!
- If your customer is moving around, then get up and move with them. (Not recommended on an actual roller coaster.)
- If your customer is angry, then get serious.
- If your customer is relaxed, then be relaxed (but still professional).
- If your customer says you have five minutes, then focus.

The moral of this story: You need to match your customer's energy and movement if you want to establish rapport. The goal is to come as close to their energy, mood, and movement as possible without coming across as fake.

Spoiler alert: If you don't already do this, you'll likely feel like a fake at first. Don't give up—listening for cues and matching your customer's energy and body language takes work but will soon become a 100-percent natural part of you. *Namaste. Thank you for attending my sales yoga retreat.*

4. Appear confident

Ah, confidence. Synonyms for this word are *trust, faith, belief,* and *certainty*—heavy words, but let's not overcomplicate this one. As a relationship manager, confidence means:

- Trusting yourself in any situation.
- Having faith in your ideas, products, people, services, and work.
- Speaking with certainty.
- Carrying an unshakable belief that you know your stuff (while being real about what you don't know—don't bullsh*t yourself or your customer).

Most salespeople have some degree of natural self-confidence. If your chosen profession requires getting another human being to part with their money, you have to have *some* percentage of faith in yourself (no matter how small that percentage might be). It's the salesperson who couples their natural self-confidence with aptitude and self-awareness who is a cut above the rest.

These are the salespeople who never stop practicing and preparing. Ever heard of a professional athlete who stops practicing after turning pro? Neither have I! But how does confidence play a role in creating rapport?

Glad you asked. Before any sales meeting, I review my notes (taking stock of where I am in my sales process and looking to what's next), brush up on the company and/or individual I am meeting with, and research any outside factors that could potentially arise (market information, competitors, raw materials, etc.). I know from personal experience that increasing confidence is directly tied to *personal preparation and organization*—the #1 item on the rapport-building list. It worked for me, and it will work for you.

Preparing and organizing sounds easy enough, right? It truly is, but salespeople too often overlook or take for granted this important component of rapport-building.

Let me share a wake-up call about confidence from early in my career.

I had to inform one of my best customers about a substantial price increase. My company had enjoyed this business for years, and the customer/owner (my main contact) and I had great rapport. I set a meeting and prepared to speak to the increase in the exact language the company provided. I was confident!

The owner was prepared, too. Analytical, he studied markets daily, and the Harvard MBA diploma hanging in his office is now forever burned into my brain. Though I knew all this, somehow I never thought about conducting my own research into historical market peaks and valleys—you know, the same information the customer could (would) use to combat the increase. (If you're anticipating the train that was barreling down the tracks toward me, you're ahead of where I was.)

I was blissfully overconfident. Looking back, I can see that I took our relationship and their loyalty for granted.

The day of our meeting, I presented my reasons for the increase and expected my customer to accept them. He did not. Instead, he hit me with five or 10 years of raw data supporting his position and sent me packing. I walked to my car with my tail between my legs.

After a few hours of painful self-reflection (and some sulking, let's be real), I recognized the experience as a timely slice of humble pie that showed me the value of preparation and the proper degree of self-confidence.

I rebounded more determined than ever to negotiate this increase. Like the Terminator, I knew I'd be back. Using their data and my own research, I prepared a new increase and rehearsed its presentation. I now had an evidence-based, unshakeable belief in my proposal, and I could speak with certainty tempered by the humility that came from having my ass handed to me. This time, he accepted my increase. (David, if you're reading this, thanks for the huge and much-needed lesson. Sincerely.)

Moral of the story: Prepare and be confident, but know when to retreat and regroup. Confidence and preparation go hand in hand; confidence without preparation is the easiest way to come off as cocky, uneducated, uncaring, wrong—and makes rapport-building impossible.

5. Focus on the customer

It's not about you until it is, and it's definitely not about you in the beginning. To build rapport, the bulk of your customer interactions should involve them talking and you listening. It's pretty hard to discover anything other than a blatantly obvious need when you're the one talking the most.

I remember thinking I had to spew every company and widget factoid in my head immediately on meeting a new prospect. How would they know how great we were if I didn't instantly tell them? Those first sales calls had to have been painful for my customers. A heartfelt apology to all those people; it was me, not you.

Firehosing capabilities and features at your customer is the wrong approach to building rapport. Your goal is to get the customer talking, and I don't mean talking about *the fish*. Focusing on the customer looks like this:

1. You say you want to learn about their _____ (operation, business, process, etc.).
2. You ask a mix of open- (mostly) and closed-ended questions designed to get them talking about _____.
3. You give them all the runway in the world to respond.
4. They hear and see check-ins, or reflections, from you along the way.
5. They're talking 75 percent of the time, you 25 percent of the time.
6. You maintain good eye contact, taking brief notes as needed.

(As a brief class refresher, closed-ended questions are appropriate when you want to get measurable data or a yes/no answer; open-ended questions allow the respondent the freedom to answer as they like and supply details that can be valuable to the questioner.)

Early on, when the bulk of rapport-building takes place, you have an important objective: Your customer speaks more than you. Period. If Yoda was a sales coach, he might say, "Listen, you must. A solution offered without a need is the quickest path to the dark side."

6. Listen and reflect

We'll spend the next chapter on reflecting and continue to talk about it throughout the book, but a preview here is warranted. "Listen and reflect" builds off our previous PSC principle, "focus on the customer," and ties in nicely with the figures I just gave you: If you are talking only 25 percent of the time, then you must be listening the other 75 percent, right? Yes, but what listening sounds like might surprise you (and "sounds like" was not a typo). **Listening does have a sound.** Let that sink in for a second. While your customer is speaking, listening is the sound of you checking in at appropriate times to confirm your understanding and providing more runway for the speaker to continue. This is contrary to your third grade teacher's definition of listening, *the sound of silence*, and Simon & Garfunkel's 1964 hit song by the same name.

We're going to deconstruct the sound of listening in the next chapter. For now, the (abbreviated) steps that lead to a reflection are:

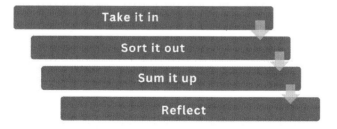

Take it in: You are listening physically; their words are entering your ears and ultimately landing in your brain (scientific, I know).

Sort it out: Sounds, words, and sentences are floating around in your brain; you start to separate words/ideas into buckets (major themes).

Sum it up: You put a central theme into your own words. I can't stress this enough—*your own words.*

Reflect: You find an appropriate (read: unforced) pause in the conversation to offer a quick interpretation of one of your customer's themes without judgment. Repeat periodically. Each reflection:

1. helps you gauge your level of understanding,
2. lets the speaker know you are actively listening and truly understanding,
3. gives the speaker a green light to keep talking, to go deeper, and
4. builds rapport.

We just looked at reflecting from 30,000 feet. Now, get excited—we're about to dive in (or soar higher, really, given the altitude analogy)—much deeper and higher!

There's a lot here to digest, and there should be. Building rapport (trust and credibility) is not achieved overnight, and it definitely has nothing to do with that *thing* hanging in your customer's office. Real rapport is about preparation and being in tune with the customer's learning style(s). It's built by going on that roller coaster ride we spoke of and appearing confident (without bullsh*tting yourself or the customer). What they are saying is most important, not what you feel like you need to say. Your questions matter greatly when building rapport, and your ability to reflect matters just as much.

Take your time, practice these skills, and try skipping *the fish*. (OK, I know I said a tiny, tiny bit of *the fish* is allowed, but only a morsel.) If you happen to like the same things as your customer, call that a bonus.

REFLECT

4

Reflecting
The sound of listening

"Listening has a sound." I made this statement in the last chapter, and I stand by it 100 percent. I must admit, though, that if I had shared this concept with my children as I wrote this book, my then-7-year-old would have glee-fully told me I sounded crazy; my 10-year-old would have followed up with, "You don't get it, Dad. Listening is quiet."

I used to believe that, too.

Here's the deal: As it relates to the demystification of sales (or relationships/parenting/life) success, reflecting is the sound of listening. Put another way, it is the manifestation of active listening.

REFLECTING (OR THE MORE GENERAL TERM, ACTIVE LISTENING) IS THE SECRET TO NEXT-LEVEL SALES. In a 2016 article[1] published in *Harvard Business Review* authors Jack Zenger and Alex Folkman revealed four characteristics common to next-level listeners. To paraphrase:

1. **The best listeners ask constructive questions that spark deeper conversation.**
   So we can officially graduate from our grade school definition of listening. Harvard said so.

2. **The speaker should walk away feeling good about the interaction.**
   Telling the listener something should be a positive experience for the speaker.

3. **The interaction sounds like a healthy back-and-forth; the listener is not (deliberately) attempting to poke holes in the speaker's story.**
   It should feel as if the conversation was an act of co-construction.

4. **Good listeners earn the right to render advice.**
   Suggestions typically make speakers feel as if the listener is solving rather than listening (as I did for my wife), but people might be more receptive to advice or a challenge from those who embody points 1-3.

See how reflecting is the sound of listening? It's not silence. As we said in the last chapter, while your customer is speaking, listening is the sound of you checking in at

---

1 https://hbr.org/2016/07/what-great-listeners-actually-do, accessed 4 January 2024.

appropriate times to confirm your understanding and providing more runway for the speaker to continue.

Reflecting isn't quiet nodding. Reflecting is active and helps us properly break our teacher-and-parent-imbued listener silence. When done right, reflecting earns us the right to probe, challenge, and ask more questions.

Here's another opportunity for lesser salespeople to fall short. If you consider rapport-building as a single stage (OK, check! Done.), then you're likely to stop (or maybe never even start) reflecting, too. However, stellar salespeople reflect during every part of PSC, not just during rapport-building. Little to no reflecting during every stage of in-person or virtual customer-facing sales interactions typically kills a relationship (or keeps one from forming). The absence of reflecting is why so many salespeople wail some form of, "I just can't get this prospect to open up. I can't get them to talk!" I've made that statement myself in the past. News flash: They might be talking while you aren't really listening … or they may realize you're not listening and so won't waste their time.

Remember, PSC comprises the principles and steps you use to build a relationship, uncover a need, propose a solution, sell your products or services, and ultimately save or make the customer money. Reflecting, *the act of active listening,* is so vital to the process that we could, and should, make this simple addition to every step:

1. Build rapport + *reflect*
2. Understand needs + *reflect*
3. Deliver solutions + *reflect*
4. Close the interaction + *reflect*

We have referred to those four steps, or stages of PSC, as a relationship process, but we could just as easily refer to them as a communication process; *how* we communicate during the process is just as important as the steps themselves. Reflecting is integral to great customer-salesperson communication. If appropriate reflecting is absent at any point, the effectiveness of each step is greatly diminished or lost completely. Anyone can follow steps, but only by perfecting the principles and skills within the steps will you go to the next level. And since you're motivated enough to read this book, I know you can achieve that level.

THREE BIG TAKEAWAYS:

1. Reflecting is the act of active listening—the sound of listening.
2. Suitable reflecting yields superior two-way communication.
3. In sales, real listening requires reflecting.

WHAT REFLECTION SOUNDS LIKE IN CONVERSATION

In the previous chapter, I shared this preview of reflecting: While your customer is speaking, listening is the sound of you checking in at appropriate times to confirm your understanding and providing more runway for the speaker to continue. Let's strip it down now so it can really sink in. Recall that the simplified formula looks like this:

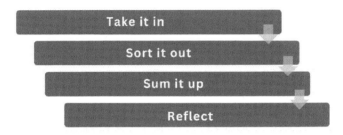

Here is an example of what my reflection might sound like in talking with a customer:

Customer: "Your cost is much higher than I expected." Suitable reflection: "It sounds like a low acquisition price is important to you right now."

What makes this a good reflection?

1. **Take it in.**
I did what most anyone would consider listening: The words physically entered my ears and then magically landed in my mind (apologies to any neuroscientists). So yes, I took in the words being said by the customer.

2. **Sort it out.**
I latched onto two words that were the meat of what the customer said: *cost* and *higher*. I sorted out what I was hearing.

3. **Sum it up.**
I found suitable words to convey my understanding. First, the prospect incorrectly used the word *cost*.

In value selling, *cost* is typically married with the value associated with an object or service (usually over time). I'm glad they used this word; my mind instantly substituted it with **price**, which is actually what they meant. *Price,* or *acquisition price,* is what we pay upfront to acquire an item or service. As for the word *higher,* since I shifted the original definition by using *price,* I now needed to substitute *higher* with **low** to make this reflection make sense. Notice I said *substitute*; this is an important point—I'm using my own words, not just parroting theirs.

4. Reflect.

I would wait for a natural pause in our conversation to make my reflection, sooner rather than later since it appeared to denote a big red flag for the customer.

"It sounds like a low acquisition price is important to you right now."

The customer would probably respond with, "Exactly!" or "It sure is, but value is equally important. Price isn't everything."

If I'm glad to hear that first response, which I am, the second one is pure gold! First, the word *exactly* is one of my favorites because it tells you they genuinely feel heard, which means you made a huge deposit in their emotional bank account. In the second response, the customer is keying in on the fact that you reflected what's most important to them and, in the same breath, they are giving you more detailed information to work from. That's a big moment for a salesperson; the door for a value-based conversation is swinging wide open! All thanks to a solid reflection.

It's worth noting that reflections can take on one of two personalities: (1) they convey exactly what was said, or (2) they convey what we think the speaker meant to say. Either version is a reflection; it's up to you to decide when to use which one. My reflection above fits into the latter category, which can be more difficult when first applying the skill of reflecting. When starting out, work on conveying exactly what was said.

Now that we have the basics, let's go step-by-step once more but cover a few of the finer details of the reflection formula:

1. Take it in.
   a. A talkative client can be a goldmine by providing you with useful detail, *if* you are able to sort and retain the most valuable pieces.
   b. If they happen to be prattling on about *the fish*, it's your job to politely and smoothly transition to a subject more closely related to why you asked for (and they agreed to) the meeting.

2. Sort it out.
   a. You are flagging information that might be significant so you can recall it within a few minutes, and ditching what you won't necessarily need to keep brain space free.
   b. In simple terms, you're making snap judgments about every word at lightning speed. Remember Willy Wonka's device that could instantly sort

the good golden goose eggs from the bad? Just like that device, you have to hang onto the good information and discard the bad (less meaningful) down the shoot.

3. Sum it up.

   a. When you've sorted out a telling detail, you need to put it in your own words before reflecting it back; this simply means finding a synonym. *Maintenance* becomes *upkeep*, *vehicles* and *properties* become *assets*, *regulated* becomes *governed*.

   b. The most important advice I can give here is to not overthink this step. When new to reflecting, we tend to overanalyze our word choices. Don't. Find logical, basic substitutes for your reflection.

4. Reflect.

   a. Wait for a natural pause from your speaker to make your reflection.

   b. Use *you*, *your*, and *you're*. This will help you understand (and show your understanding of) the speaker's point of view.

      "You think ..." – reflecting a thought.
      "You sound ..." – reflecting a feeling.
      "You sound ... because ..." – reflecting feelings and thoughts.

   c. The biggest mistake people make here is letting a reflection sound like a question because their voice changes pitch. Reflections, by their very nature, are *implied* questions, so there is no need to change your tone of voice on the last word, adding that verbal question mark. If you raise your tone of voice at the end of a sentence, you become a prosecuting attorney grilling a witness. Say it with me: "Reflections are statements, not questions."

d. You might feel like you're forcing something the first few times you reflect. If you feel uncomfortable, just keep at it. Reflecting is a skill, and a skill must be practiced. And now that I've scared you, let me ask a favor: Don't knock it 'til you've tried it. I guarantee this: The first time you hear "Exactly!" in response to one of your reflections, you'll feel like a master yourself.

e. "Reflecting sounds fake." I've heard this statement more times than I can count, always from people new to the formal concept. I say *formal* because we've all experienced reflecting; it's just never been given a name. If you can recall a time when you told a story and felt truly heard, your listener was reflecting, I promise you.

f. You don't reflect everything you hear. If you do, you will indeed sound fake (or crazy).

To tie a bow on our initial look at listening/reflecting, let me quote Jane again: "Listening is a skill that demonstrates an understanding of the customer's thoughts and feelings from the customer's frame of reference." Two things to call out in this nugget:

1. Listening is a skill—and any skill must be practiced.
2. Listening is not simply hearing—it is demonstrating understanding.

In summary, let's look at the big-picture benefits of next-level listening (reflecting) in sales, as defined by PSC:

1. Your listening delivers the goods, accurately uncovering the customer's business concerns, needs, and issues.
2. Your listening helps the customer stay on track (you are attempting to keep them on a specific topic).
3. Your listening allows you to clarify and verify information about the customer's situation.
4. Your listening brings the customer on a shared journey with you, one where they participate and build ownership in your forthcoming recommendations and solutions.

In the next chapter, we'll discuss barriers to communication because if we're not careful, these barriers can creep into our client-facing speech when we should be reflecting. If you are like I was, you erect some of these barriers today, likely unbeknownst to you. But have no fear—we'll knock down these walls of words, hopefully crushing some of your bad habits. We're just getting warmed up!

BEFORE WE CLOSE THIS CHAPTER, IT'S YOUR TURN TO DO SOME LISTENING AND REFLECTING.

Assume you just heard a customer make the statements below, and write down your reflections. I'll share mine in the next chapter, and we'll compare notes. Two things I ask: (1) please do the exercise—I don't want you to cheat yourself of the experience, and (2) don't look ahead at my reflections until you complete yours.

Write down your reflections to these statements:

1. "Your service is terrible. I never know when you're coming, and when I do know, you're late." (The speaker's tone is elevated and unpleasant.)
2. "Your company is killing it! I'm so happy I switched my business to you." (The speaker's tone is light and excited.)
3. "I'm at the end of my rope with product failures. They're starting to impact our production." (The speaker's tone is serious and matter-of-fact.)
4. "My team is a wreck right now. We lack direction—we're all over the place. We'll never make our numbers." (The speaker's tone is pure frustration.)

Happy reflecting!

5

Barriers to Sales Communication
We can be our own worst enemies

Evaluation time! If you've finished your assignment from Chapter 4, let's compare them to my reflections to those same five statements. If you haven't done the exercise, please take time now to do so; you'll get so much more out of this chapter.

1. **Customer statement: "Your service is terrible. I never know when you're coming, and when I do**

know, you're late." (The speaker's tone is elevated and unpleasant.)

My reflections: My tone will be concerned and matter-of-fact, slightly elevated to meet their level of displeasure. I will not raise my voice at the end of my sentences.

- "We're really dropping the ball."
- "You're not happy with our performance."
- "It sounds like our delivery is marginal, at best."

Common barrier responses from salespeople:

- "I find this hard to believe." (Agree/disagree)
- "Do you have data to support these claims?" (Questioning)
- "Several factors are working against us here." (Logic)
- "We'll get better. You have my word on it." (Reassurance)

How did your reflections compare with mine? Did any barriers sneak in? Most people lean on *questioning* and *reassurance* when hit with a harsh critique like the one above—you naturally want to probe to defend yourself and say it will never happen again. Fight that urge. A reflection will allow you to take ownership of the situation and disarm your speaker (to some degree). They will continue to empty their bucket, but their tone and displeasure should start to lessen.

2. **Customer statement: "Your company is killing it! I'm so happy I switched my business to you."** (The speaker's tone is light and excited.)

My reflections: My tone will be appreciative/humble but include some pep. I won't raise my voice at the end of my sentences/sound like a question.

- "You're loving us right now!"
- "It sounds like we are delivering!"
- "I'm hearing no buyer's remorse!"

Notice that all three of my reflections included exclamation points. I intentionally inserted them to convey my overall excitement level in this case. Instead of raising my voice at one particular point, I elevated my tone for the entire sentence. They were excited about something positive, and I met them on their level.

Common barrier responses from salespeople:

- "You are the one who deserves all the credit." (Praising)
- "First off, I would like to thank God, my agent, and the Academy ..." (Monologue)

How did your reflections compare with mine? Any barriers? Truth be told, not a lot of barriers intrude when receiving positive feedback. The two most common are *praising* (giving credit right back to them) and a *monologue* (your "Academy Awards" acceptance speech). Enjoy the praise, own it, and reflect it back to your customer.

3. **Customer statement: "I'm at the end of my rope with product failures. They're starting to impact our production."**

(The speaker's tone is serious and matter-of-fact.)

My reflections: My tone is serious and steady.

- "Your business is starting to suffer."
- "The product is not holding up in your application."
- "It sounds like you're at a loss."

Common barrier responses from salespeople:

- "Switch your current buy to _____, and this will be a non-issue." (Advising)
- "All the signs point to a clear root cause." (Logic)
- "Are you sure your team is using the product correctly?" (Questioning)
- "We will make the proper changes, and this will never happen again." (Reassurance)

How did your reflections compare with mine? Did any barriers creep in? The two most common barriers in this situation are *questioning* (you know you can solve the puzzle if you just get the right questions out) and *reassurance* (you can fix the problem and desperately want to tell them so). Reflections in this case build credibility ... you're taking the time to acknowledge that the customer has a serious issue before moving on. If they want to go deeper, you've given them the runway to do so.

4. **Customer statement: "My team is a wreck right now. We lack direction—we're all over the place. We'll never make our numbers."** (The speaker's tone is pure frustration.)

   My reflections: My tone is empathetic, genuinely concerned and steady.

   - "Your team is a mess."
   - "You're worried you won't make your goal."
   - "Success is not sounding attainable."

   Common barrier responses from salespeople:

   - "Who is the weak link in this equation?" (Questioning)
   - "If anyone can bring this team together, it's you." (Praising)
   - "You need to take charge of the situation." (Advising)
   - "You think you have it bad, well, you should see our results—my team is the real train wreck." (Diverting)

How did your reflections compare with mine? What about barriers? The three most common barriers that sneak into situations like this are *advising* (you are quick to share your opinion on a way forward), *praising* (you want to say they're just the person to turn this thing around), and *questioning* (we're dying to ask that one perfect question to help us solve their problem). Frustration is one of the best things you can reflect. Just like in our personal lives, we humans need to let it out (think pressure cooker ready to blow). Reflections can help to slowly alleviate pressure that has built up … avoiding the explosion.

How did you do? Having taught hundreds of salespeople using a similar exercise in person, I can tell you that well over 75 percent of my students fail initially. But already armed with the mechanics of how to reflect, my hope is that you did better than they typically do. I was rooting for you!

In a live setting, I don't initially define what it means to reflect. Instead, I start with an exercise to prove that the untrained salesperson typically falls back on barrier responses. I go around the room making statements that their customers might make and ask individuals to respond on the fly, in front of their peers. And I intentionally use the word "respond" because I am trying to get their most natural reactions to things their customers might say. In actuality, I'm bracing myself to hear their barrier responses.

I use this as an introduction to reflecting in a live setting because it tells a powerful story … That if untrained, we unconsciously rely heavily on barrier responses in the vast majority of our conversations. We unintentionally build barriers that make meaningful communication almost impossible.

Below, I've laid out the most common 11 barriers we unintentionally throw in our own way.

11 COMMON BARRIERS TO MEANINGFUL COMMUNICATION

- **Agree/Disagree:** "What a horrible problem!" or "That's not so important."
- **Blame:** "You always seem to ..."
- **Praising:** "You're a great problem solver—you handle it."
- **Advising:** "I think you should ..."
- **Monologue:** "Blah, blah, blah, blah ..."
- **Logic:** "Several symptoms are clear ..."
- **Moralizing:** "People in this company will always ..."
- **Ordering:** "If you don't ... you can expect ..."
- **Diverting:** "You think you have it bad ..."
- **Reassuring:** "Things will really look different tomorrow."
- **Questioning (the champion of barriers):** "Did you ... have you ... how come ... where ... how much ...?"

The undisputed champion of barrier responses, based on my classroom exercise: *Questioning.* Why? Because salespeople are trained to solve problems.

PSC Sage Advice: The minute we salespeople hear a problem, we should fight the urge to ask questions with every fiber of our being, at least initially. We should look to reflect instead.

Hear me out. Questions can quickly become barriers. Fact. But questioning has its place, and wanting to problem-solve is not inherently a bad trait. Where salespeople really go off the rails with questioning is related to *timing.*

When a customer is still venting or describing a challenge isn't the time to solve their problem. As we discussed earlier, you have not yet earned this right. Think about this: Have you ever tried to solve your significant other's problem in the middle of its airing? If so, you've undoubtedly crashed and burned more often than not; they might want your help, but not until they get things off their chest *and feel heard*. (Me. My wife. Early in our marriage.)

You must ask questions to engage in discovery, of course; that's gospel, law, Do Not Pass Go, Do Not Collect $200. You need questions. But interjecting in the middle of the speaker's story comes across as interrogation. The more you question/agree/disagree/toss out barrier responses (a.k.a. *judge*), the less the speaker will talk.

Why would voicing a reflection instead of a question change the outcome here? The two biggest reasons:

1. reflecting is nonjudgmental, and
2. reflecting allows the speaker to empty their bucket, which we've touched on before.

Incorrectly timed questions sound like judgment, and we all want to tell a story without feeling judged in real time for the content.

LET THEM EMPTY THEIR BUCKET

I can't address avoiding barriers to emptying a customer's bucket without referring to my mentor Scott Crandall. To drive the point home, Scott had us envision a red plastic bucket full of horse manure. He could've picked a bucket of popcorn or something less cringe-inducing (you can smell it, right?), but would the image (and smell) have stuck with us? He knew what he was doing when he picked this visual! I still remember his words, which I paraphrase below, and I encourage you to embrace the thought of assisting a customer with emptying their bucket (of horse manure). Here's why:

If we visualize a story (or challenge) as something contained within a bucket, we can imagine deep, unseen layers. The top reveals only surface-level details and emotions but not a ton of facts. Chances are, the part of the story we salespeople need to hear is all the way at the bottom. That's where the juicy stuff (sorry!) is buried—the pain point to address. By *reflecting*, we can thoughtfully dig our way through the bucket's contents, gently surfacing details from the speaker. Get the point? If you don't let someone empty their bucket, you likely will miss out on the real issue … and you'll leave a customer still holding their bucket of s**t … a bucket filled with valuable details and nuggets (again, sorry!) that you missed.

Reflecting is the key to emptying someone's bucket. If you feel stuck in discovery with a customer, you haven't reflected in a way that has helped them empty their bucket.

THE TRAINING WHEELS OF REFLECTING: "IT SOUNDS LIKE …"

One or two things have likely happened as you read this chapter: (1) Your mind is already thinking in terms of reflections, and/or (2) the idea of asking questions during a sales call now terrifies you. Have no fear! We'll cover the art of questioning in the next chapter, as we learn how to apply our new reflecting skills to understanding needs. The pieces of PSC are coming together!

Reflecting can be awkward at first. If you struggle with being direct with your reflections, using "you/your/you're" as suggested in the previous chapter, try starting your reflections with, "It sounds like." I like to refer to "it sounds like" as *the training wheels of reflecting.* "It sounds like … " leads you right down the path toward a natural-sounding reflection, typically keeping you clear of the dreaded question. Put these training wheels on if you can't initially steer clear of barrier responses—they will keep you upright and reflecting!

As you hone your reflecting skills, you will see benefits in *all* aspects of your life. If you are a parent, reflecting can fend off meltdowns and fights, and help everyone in your family feel heard. The sales benefits are profoundly similar. Reflecting gives your customers the *green light* and *runway* needed to keep talking, to keep emptying their emotional and factual buckets, all while you build rapport and engage in awesome discovery.

HOMEWORK

Try out reflecting on family and friends tonight or this weekend. Reflecting lighthearted conversation is a great way to get comfortable with this powerful communication tool.

If your spouse/partner/friend says, "I can't wait for Friday!" respond with, "It sounds like you are ready for the weekend!" and note what happens.

REFLECT

6

Understanding Needs
Can we ask questions now?

You have their attention. You landed the first big meeting with your customer. Now what? It's time to find and fully understand a need to fulfill, a pain point to relieve, or a place to partner.

If you recall from previous chapters, understanding needs is the second step in PSC.

1. Build rapport
2. **Understand needs**

3. Deliver solutions

4. Close the interaction

In most sales processes, this step or action is referred to as *discovery*, a universally accepted term to describe how we go about understanding and assessing customer needs. Used in all types of B2B sales, from marketing to outside sales, it's the longest part of any sales process. Finding the right problem to solve for your customer (while building rapport, of course) can take a while, especially in relationship sales. Think of it like meeting that special someone. Courtship is really just discovering things about each other: Do they chew with their mouth open, are they kind to strangers, do they have an extra toe, do they regularly call their mother, were they once part of an amateur circus, do they speed into intersections, etc. So. Many. Questions. No kidding, ask dates about circus experience. Trust me.

In the Todd Phillips' Vegas-based film *The Hangover*, Stu (Ed Helms' lovable, emotional character) meets Jade (played by a carefree Heather Graham) and marries her after minimal discovery: 12 hours of excitement. Spoiler alert: The dire need for annulment comes up the very next day. The lesson applies to sales: As much as we would like to find and understand our customer's needs in a single meeting, chances are it's not going to, and shouldn't, happen that quickly. Relationships that lead to uncovering true needs and long-term customer loyalty take time. (I was really pulling for Stu and Jade, though!)

Just like our Vegas lovebirds should have, we need to ask the right questions. There's no other way to accurately *reflect* back to your customer, right (you master reflector, you)?

The art and science of asking questions often doesn't get the attention (or respect) it deserves. Many see it as a universal truth that we are going to ask questions during discovery and that everyone inherently knows how to ask them. I hear, "Of course we ask questions; I was born at night, but not last night." But by now, you know there is more to it. A lot more than simply ending a string of words with a question mark.

PSC details five key benefits to purposeful questioning.

Through purposeful questioning, we:

1. accurately uncover the customer's critical concerns, needs, and issues,
2. gather and verify information about the customer's situation vs. the assumptions we made or will make,
3. glean information that relates to the customer's decision-making criteria,
4. clarify what's essential to creating a clear value proposition for our products/services that is 100-percent aligned to the customer's business issues, and
5. gain the opportunity to revisit things we do not fully understand.

Gathering relevant information is job #1, but allow me to key in on a couple of words: ***verify and aligned***. I don't know about you, but I think those words carry deeply significant meanings for sales. Let's look at each idea in turn.

- **Verify**

Related to being accurate, there is zero shame in verifying you heard a fact correctly. The shame will come if you base your proposal off something you misheard. If you think you might have gotten something wrong, you probably did. Clarify and verify.

- **Aligned**

You're looking to align your products or services with their business needs. Delivering aligned solutions (a later step in PSC) should sound like this: "Because we both agreed that _____ was a need, I am proposing _____ [aligned solution]."

KEY ELEMENTS OF GREAT QUESTIONING

Just like reflecting, questioning is a skill you must practice. If you are not constantly honing and reinforcing your questioning muscle memory, you can lose your touch. For me, I'm sharper when I have a full pipeline; I'm celebrating my discovery wins and learning from my mistakes, applying winning techniques from one discovery session and leaving bad ones behind in the next. The more I find myself in the hunt, the better I am. You might feel just the opposite, feeling more confident as you drill into one specific opportunity at a time. To paraphrase Monty Python, we are all individuals who think for ourselves. You do you!

Questions are individual, too, and not all are created equal. PSC lists five key elements to fruitful discovery:

1. Use both open- and closed-ended questions.
2. Ask purposeful/limited questions.
3. Preface questions where appropriate.

4. Follow with a reflection of their answer (you knew that was coming!).
5. End with a situational summary.

1. Use both open- and closed-ended questions. (Refer back to chapter 3 if you need a refresher on definitions.) Open-ended questions are the gold standard in questioning—they get the speaker going on a topic you steered them into and typically yield amazing bits of information. The beauty of this technique: You're simply giving the customer a topic to talk on that interests them as well as you.

Here's an example: To learn more about the time a customer was in the circus (just go with me for a second here), a great open-ended question would be, "What was life like in the circus; can you tell me about a typical weekend?" Chances are, you'll get colorful details and useful nuggets of information. Want to ask an open-ended question without even asking a question? You can make a request instead: "Tell me what life was like in the circus; I'd love to hear about a typical weekend." If that feels unnatural to you, that's ok, the almighty question mark is always there for you.

Surprised that I included closed-ended questions? They do have a place in understanding needs.

To ask a closed-ended question initially in this scenario sets you up for a conversation killer: "How long were you in the circus?" "Three years." "Did you enjoy it?" "Yes." Those questions are as closed as a Chick-fil-A on a Sunday, boring and not conducive to natural interaction. Closed-ended questions are reserved for follow-up data collection; you've asked a great open-ended question, your customer has provided tons of detail, but you sense/feel/know that an important fact or figure is missing. If a reflection or two does not produce all the information you need, then a clarifying closed-ended question like, "How long were you in the circus?" fits here. A good way to approach questioning is open first, closed later.

2. Ask purposeful/limited questions. Though this should go without saying, I have to reiterate: Your questions should have a purpose. Remember *the fish*? Fish talk is the opposite of purposeful. You should also not be afraid to prompt a limit to the information you are seeking.

Think about it like this: If your open-ended question provides a specific road for the speaker to travel down (the overarching topic), then limits built into your question will act as guard rails to keep them from veering off on a tangent. Keeping with my circus theme (strange, but hopefully memorable): Assuming my purpose was to uncover more about the twilight of this person's circus career and their transition into business, a question/request with limits might sound like, "Tell me about the end of your time in the circus and the transition you made to becoming a business owner." It's open-ended but also limited, as I've asked about a very specific time period.

3. Preface a group of questions where appropriate. To preface a group of questions is like setting an overall theme. You might say, "I sense a connection between your time in the circus and where you are now; if it's ok with you, I'd like to really hone in on that time period with a few questions." With that, you've just asked for permission to get laser-focused on one topic (yup, more circus). Similar to imposing limits (think one question at a time), a preface is there to put a boundary around a group of questions you are about to serve up.

A well-delivered prefacing statement can set some intentional limits right out of the gate, without you having to work them question by question. It lets the customer know why you need the information for which you are asking and how divulging that information could potentially help them. My approach is to preface with each topic change, when possible.

You know you did an amazing job in prefacing if your customer responds with, "What would you like to know?"

4. Follow with a reflection of their answer. If reflecting were a dead horse, this is where you'd think I was beating it, so I'll just refer you to earlier chapters if you need a reflecting refresher. I'll just say this: Offer natural reflections to the speaker's responses, but remember, don't reflect every single thing—it sounds weird. You got this!

5. End with a situational summary. You may recall from high school the formula for successful public speaking (Vito's formula referenced earlier): (1) tell them what you're about to tell them, (2) tell them, (3) tell them what you told them. A situational summary is the third component of that formula. Whether a quick recap of a conversation and/or next steps, ending with a summary is always a great idea. Depending on how long you conversed with the speaker, rarely should this ever be longer than a minute or two in duration. You're stating, "This is what I heard you say and this is where I think we are headed next." This also allows the speaker a chance to affirm that you are on the right track.

AVOIDING INTERROGATION, THE MOTHER OF ALL QUESTIONING PITFALLS

There is one pitfall of questioning that we must address. Poorly prefaced, timed, and crafted questions can make your customer feel interrogated. This is not news to you; you've heard this fact before, and chances are you have even done some interrogating yourself (I sure did, early on). When I think back to some of my first discovery sessions selling commercial truck tires, interrogation sounded like this: "How many trucks do you run? How many trailers are in the fleet? On average, how many miles does one of your trucks run in a year? Who is your tire manufacturer of choice? Are you happy with them? Do you track fuel economy?"

Bad, bad, bad. We've all received a volley of questions like this, and it always felt like interrogation. It sounds like zero prefacing, then one closed-ended question after another until the customer is answering like a police suspect under a bright light. Therapy moment: If your discovery sessions sound like this, it's time for a change. Think back to my (hopefully) memorable circus examples!

So, in summary:

- purposeful discovery with prefaced—mostly open-ended—questions = good,
- interrogation (all closed) = bad.

To avoid interrogation, mix up the four question types in your reflecting:

1. General discovery questions
2. Perceived need questions
3. Impact questions
4. Possible outcome questions

1. General discovery questions are there to help us gather big-picture information. Think along the lines of my circus questions. Getting the lay of the land is an essential part of most sales calls, especially during early discovery. You are not necessarily looking for a problem here, but a general understanding of the customer. We're going for the big open-ended questions/requests:

- I'd love to hear about your core business. What do you _____ (build, grow, make, service, transport, etc.)?
- Tell me about your operation/department.
- Let's discuss what you are currently doing in regard to _____.

2. Perceived need questions relate to what you as the salesperson believe (or perceive) are your customer's needs, problems, and outcomes: You ask questions to ensure you understand these correctly and confirm the customer's expectations of a product, service, salesperson, and company:

- What are you trying to accomplish?
- What problems are you having now?
- What do you want to change? What could be better?
- What would you consider a high priority right now?
- How can my company make a difference?
- If you could design the perfect _____, what would you include?
- What would you fine-tune with your _____?

- What are the disadvantages of the way you're handling this now?
- What do you see as your biggest challenges in the coming year?

3. Impact questions aim at uncovering possible losses or negative consequences of not acting:
- If your _____ needs are not adequately met, how will this impact you?
- If you don't act, what happens?
- What's your greatest frustration regarding _____?
- Why would you find [solution] so useful?
- What happens if you don't solve this problem?
- What difficulties does this problem create for you? How far-reaching is its impact?
- What problems will be created for you if you don't receive the kind of service you expect?

4. Possible outcome questions focus on expectations, hopes, goals, and plans. These concentrate the customer's attention on the potential solution rather than the current problem, creating a positive, problem-solving atmosphere focused on action:
- How do you think a first-rate _____ could help?
- What are your future plans? What's next?
- What are your goals/expectations for _____?
- What are you going to gain by solving this problem/accomplishing this goal?
- How would you describe the ideal _____?
- In a nutshell, what do you expect from _____?

- By this time next year, where do you want to be with _____?
- What would be the benefits of getting the kind of _____ you're looking for?

I led by saying that understanding needs (discovery) is typically the longest part of any sales process. And that's not a bad thing. However long discovery takes, enjoy your thorough fact-finding because it will set you up for solutions perfectly aligned to the customer's business needs, with minimal negotiation. To put a bow on understanding needs, I quote one of Jane's most sage pieces of advice: "If possible, do not cease with questions until you fully understand the issues."

A FINAL [RAPIDLY FLASHING RED] WARNING ABOUT QUESTIONS

In his bestselling book, "Blink: The Power of Thinking Without Thinking," Malcolm Gladwell tackles the idea that we often instantly believe we know the answers to questions that fall within our realm of expertise, sometimes within the blink of an eye, thanks to our repository of experiences. In our careers, most of us gain enough expertise to size up an issue and draw conclusions quickly, accurately, and with little conscious thought. These are truly amazing moments, culminating within your "holy crap, I know what I'm talking about" internal voice. Priceless feelings, my friends. Priceless.

Solving puzzles too quickly merits a word of caution, however. You may know why you immediately understand a customer's issue, but if it's too early in your relationship, the customer might not understand (or trust) how you came up with a solution so quickly. You can appear cocky, impatient, and unwilling to do the work required to find the best solution. Realizing this, you must perform a careful balancing act. You want to appear knowledgeable and engaged, so ask the right number of questions (not too few, not too many) to yield fruitful discovery and all the while build rapport.

THE CIRCUS: FULL DISCLOSURE

I once dated a young lady who was a member of her hometown's amateur circus. Didn't know there was such a thing? You can search "Peru Amateur Circus" if you don't believe me. Similar to being struck by lightning, the mathematical possibility of meeting someone who had been a circus performer has to be small, right?!? Thinking I was worldly at the ripe age of 22, I nevertheless was pretty astounded at learning this fact about her during our early courtship.

Obviously, the experience has stayed with me over the years; I can't help but use circus examples in talking about discovery questions. The topic makes me laugh to this day (in a good way), and hopefully it made the art of questioning a bit more memorable for you.

Oh, and if you're wondering, the circus did not come up in our first few conversations. The topic was a few layers down in the bucket. Happily, she never asked to saw me in half or shoot me out of a cannon. Shout out to Peru Amateur Circus! On with the show!

REFLECT

7

Planning for Sales Success
Who survives the life-or-death situations

Planning. It's the word equivalent of a sedative to the free spirit and euphoria to the analytical. Regardless of where you fit in, planning is a crucial part of sales success.

Previous chapters covered using a powerful mix of questions and reflections to uncover needs, pain points, and partnering opportunities. If conducting a meaningful discovery session is your ultimate destination, by the end of Chapter 6 you have the keys to the car and a full gas tank—but no way to know you're heading in the right direction.

Let's know where we're going, shall we? Regardless of your particular learning style, the following outline should help you plan for and visualize a discovery meeting. I have used this template to write a discovery meeting script time and time again, especially when concerned about my ability to stay laser-focused; the bigger the opportunity, the more scripting and visualizing I would do. And I don't mean scripting in the sense of sounding like a telemarketer delivering a speech designed to keep someone on the phone. I mean scripting in the form of knowing where you ultimately want a conversation to go and a plan to get there.

I'm about to hand you a plan, but as Laurence Gonzales points out in his book, "Deep Survival: Who Lives, Who Dies, and Why," individuals who know when to modify or scrap their original plans are the ones who survive life-or-death situations. Sales is a far cry from a life-or-death scenario—no one dies in sales, I hope—but since a huge sale could yield substantial financial reward and/or career longevity, the same principle applies: **Plan, follow said plan, but don't marry your plan.** If your original plan turns out to be terrible or new information presents itself during a customer interaction, don't be afraid to divorce your original plan and pivot. Successful salespeople plan for success yet master the pivot.

Gonzales dissected numerous survival case studies and landed on a few central themes, but the one around *confusion* really hit home for me. Confusion is a big killer. When people get so disoriented, hungry, and tired that confusion overwhelms them, they are helpless at death's door. Confusion plays a part in a dying sale, too. You've walked into your discovery session with a plan or agenda, not realizing that customers have plans of their own for our interactions. You're ready to control the direction of the meeting when you realize the customer wants to go another way completely. Hello, confusion! I have seen countless salespeople get disoriented in moments like this. As a manager (and observer), I've been able to play the part of a rescue helicopter helping individuals get unstuck. Unfortunately, you rarely have a second set of eyes and ears in a sales call, so it's up to you to steer clear of confusion. Understanding that you don't want to *marry your plan* in the hypothetical is one thing, but spotting the moment you should pivot takes real-life practice. Reflecting can be your salvation here.

I hear you thinking, "But, Matt, the idea of mapping out discovery feels too confined and unnatural for me." If this is you, I'm betting your go-to discovery/understanding needs technique is having no plan at all. I define this technique as shooting the (professional) sh*t and hoping something good appears. If this is your go-to game plan with a new or potential customer, I predict that you either fail at discovery (a lot) or sometimes get really lucky. Either way, you're leaving a lot on the table.

Disclaimer: I know that "shooting the sh*t" with a contact is alive and well as a sales/discovery technique. It's a bad one, but alive and well, nonetheless. Hell, I've made visits to do it—but I never counted on such a conversation to materialize anything productive. In my experience, the bigger the opportunity, the bigger the need to pre-script, plan, and outline a discovery session. It's a simple technique to set you up for success.

We'll go high-level first, then dig into the details. Here is your discovery plan outline:

DISCOVERY TEMPLATE

1. Customer greeting
2. Agenda review
3. Transition statement
4. Personal value proposition
5. Transition statement
6. Discovery & impact questions
7. Situational summary
8. Transition statement
9. Meeting close

1. **Customer greeting**
   a. Sounds like: "Thank you for meeting with me. Are we still good for 30 minutes?"
   b. Confirm their agreement.

2. **Agenda review**—*who are you and why are you there*
   a. Sounds like: "During our time together, I would like to accomplish the following:
   - briefly introduce myself,
   - explore your situation, and
   - discuss any next steps we might agree on."
   b. Confirm their agreement.

3. **Transition statement**
   a. Sounds like: "I want to spend most of this meeting hearing about you and understanding your specific situation/challenges. Before I do that, I'd like to first tell you a little about who I am and how I work with my customers."
   b. Check for any questions.

4. **Personal value proposition**
   a. Sounds like: "I pride myself on my ability to impact my customers' *total cost of ownership* as it relates to the products and services I sell. I'm fact-based and data-driven. My company, too, places so much emphasis on facts that *respect for proof* is one of our core values." If your customer happens to buy something from you that they will in turn resell, you need to talk in terms of the *total benefit of the partnership* (revenue generation, margin creation, portfolio diversification, rebates, co-branding, training, etc.).
   b. Check for any questions.

5. **Transition statement**
   a. Sounds like: "Now that you've heard about me and how I work with my clients, I'd like to learn more about you and how you would like to improve your business."

6. **Discovery & impact questions**
   a. **Prefacing** sounds like:
      - "To understand your business and your concerns, I need to dive deeper into …"

- "To offer any potential solutions, I need to hear more about your overall business and goals for this year."
- "To understand if I can help, I'd like to hear where you think I might potentially be of service."

Asking open-ended (and closed-ended, when needed) questions sounds like:

- "Tell me about three areas of your business that can significantly make or break your bottom line."
- "What is the single most important change you can make to positively impact your overall success? Any wins to report related to a recent change?"
- "If money and resources were not a factor in decision-making, what would you change about your operation tomorrow?"

7. **Situational summary**
   a. Sounds like:
      - "The main issues that are most important to you are ..."
      - "Your priorities over the next 3-5 years are ..."
      - "It's been hard to ..."
      - "Your current plan is to ..."
      - "_____ is a pain point."
      - "Whoever works with you must demonstrate the following characteristics ..."
      - "Did I miss anything?"

8. **Answer questions, handle issues and concerns**
   a. **Using reflections to capture the customer's thoughts and feelings** sounds like:
      - "You're concerned about …"
      - "You believe …"
      - "You'd like to know …"

9. **Meeting close**
   a. Sounds like:
      - "First, thank you for your time."
      - "I believe my company can help you. If you're open to it, I'd like to meet again."
      - "I'd like some time to review what we have discussed. How does a follow-up meeting in three weeks sound regarding some of the things we really focused on?"

What a simple, yet powerful outline, right? Just think about how productive you will be during your initial (and subsequent) discovery meetings using this outline. If you've always flown by the seat of your pants, get ready; I think you will be amazed at what this outline can yield. The responses from your customer might not always be black-and-white, but assuming you pre-qualified them and want to keep going with discovery, you should start to hear the good, the bad, and the ugly (GBU). As you reflect the GBU, you should see at least one central theme, weakness variable (that hopefully you can solve for), or partnership opportunity appear. This, ladies and gentlemen, is what we are after. This magical moment culminates in the situational summary—a mega reflection, really—that your trusty outline will prompt you to deliver to the customer, giving you the opportunity to address initial concerns in the moment and establish the next interaction.

You might find that you need more discovery. That's understandable—remember, we are viewing this through the lens of *relationship* sales, not competitive sales. Still, I'll bet you will have identified issues that you have fixes/improvements for right now, so you'll need to prepare properly to deliver those solutions successfully. Think short game versus long game. What can we solve now? What should we tackle later?

Looking back to Gonzales for inspiration, it's time to *plan* our communication, our pitch. The following five steps will help you plan your communication for delivering solutions.

COMMUNICATIONS PLAN FOR DELIVERING SOLUTIONS

1. **Define your objectives.**

   What does success look like? Seriously, ask yourself a simple question: If I had just made my proposal to _____, what would constitute a win? What is the positive outcome that would cause you to call your boss, best friend, significant other, partner, or spouse immediately after delivering your proposal? You know, the outcome that would make you scream, "I f-ing did it!" That's your objective.

   As I've said before, as salespeople, we can typically do only one of two major things for our customers: save them money or make them money. Therefore, define how and to what extent you will save or make them money with your solution. That thing you sell might make them safer, greener, or more efficient, but ultimately all things still end up in one of the two aforementioned buckets. We help them earn [money]. We help them save [money].

2. **Determine the style of communication needed to fit the customer. Prepare to get persuasive.**

We can apply several styles of communication to the basic forms of written, verbal, and nonverbal: impromptu, informative, motivational, instructional, and the one we'll focus on: *persuasive*, which for our purposes means to influence someone through reasoning. You should always present your solution in a persuasive style. Period. More on this in the next chapter.

3. **Analyze your audience.**

What about the learning style of your customer? We know we want to be persuasive, but how they want to be treated matters big-time. You studied learning styles during the rapport-building chapter; now it's time to incorporate the relevant one(s) into your persuasive proposal. Do you need to focus on visual, auditory, kinesthetic, reading/writing, or a combination of styles for a particular customer?

As previously highlighted, your customer is likely a combination of learning styles, with at least one dominant. Show them you "get them" by creating a proposal that truly speaks to how they like to receive information. Do this and you are sure to steer clear of the cardinal salesperson sin (besides talking too much): assuming every customer's main learning style is the same as your own. (More on this later, too.)

4. **Enhance your communication.**

We've analyzed our audience. Now what? It's time to enhance our communication with all the things that will speak directly to your customer's learning styles. What combination of facts, figures, visuals, models, samples, etc. will be needed to get that "W"? Remember, it's not about what you would want to experience as a buyer, it's about what *they* want to experience as the buyer.

5. **Prepare to deliver.**

Special forces, professional athletes, fighter pilots ... If you ask them what singular thing (besides their training and their own drive/fire to succeed) contributes the most to their ongoing success, I can guarantee you most will say preparation. As you move to deliver solutions, your preparation can (and will) make or break you. Remember the Harvard MBA-possessing owner I attempted to pass a price increase to with minimal preparation? I sure do.

In the next chapter, we will go deep into our persuasive format. If used correctly, persuasion will force you (and I mean that in the nicest way possible) to prepare for the win. Everything you bring to the table (who you are, who your company is, and your awesome solution) will be perfectly wrapped in a needs-based/value-producing package. Sound magical? It is.

Let's wrap and deliver your package, shall we? Buckle up!

REFLECT

8

Using Persuasion Like a Pro
Just like skateboarding, it's not a crime

We're friends by now, right? Sure, we are … and that means we can have a real discussion about something often thought to be taboo in sales, maybe even a little dirty. It's time we talk about *persuasion*. Luckily for us, persuasion is not a crime. It's how we will package PSC; it's how we will finally **deliver solutions** and **close the interaction**, resulting in that sought-after closed/won sale. It is the personification of PSC and very positive when used correctly! (And by the way, skateboarding is indeed a crime if "no skateboarding" is posted. My editor reminded me of that fact.)

Let's start by highlighting **three hard-and-fast rules of persuasion**:

1. People buy for their reasons, not yours.
2. To persuade is to influence, and influencing is the power of producing effects by invisible action.
3. The individual being persuaded must have a need or reason for taking the action you desire.

In Chapter 7, I defined persuasion as "the act of influencing through reasoning." This definition hits right at the heart of persuasion's place in relationship sales, even competitive sales, for that matter. A dictionary definition of persuasion, like this one from Merriam-Webster, adds the word *process*—"the process of persuading." Let's adopt their addition of "process" for something that best fits our PSC journey: *a process in which we influence through reasoning*.

This chapter details a persuasive outline, what I will refer to as the **PSC Persuasive Process** (our definition put into practical steps), for delivering customer solutions. This process was a game-changer for me, allowing me to make my first six-figure sale to one of my key targets and a sale made when a vice president from my corporate headquarters happened to be in attendance. What a rush!?! I'll walk you through that very sale using this process, breathing life into each step as we go. Get ready … we're close!

Before we get to our process though, we need to set something straight (yes, it's therapy time again). Persuasion gets an undeserved bad rep, so much so that I pointed to something criminal (albeit not heinous) in this chapter's title to drive the point home. I think the negative side of persuasion's reputation is rooted in two things: (1) buyer's remorse and (2) outright shady practices.

Buyer's remorse: We hear a salesperson's spiel and we buy … but we're soon asking ourselves, "What have I done? Why did I do that?" Which brings up the age-old question: "Do salespeople trick us?" The answer: Not often. We buy because we think it's a good idea. The guilt, self-recrimination, and litany of reasons we shouldn't have done what we did are what create some of persuasion's bad reputation. You had a reason to buy (because people buy for their reasons) and likely hit the *override button* on a variable that was screaming "not now, idiot!" In reality, it's just easier to blame someone else when we make bad decisions. This is reason number one. In contrast to this point, the PSC Persuasive Process should lead your buyer down a fact-filled road toward a guilt-free decision!

To help illustrate reason number two, outright shady practices, I highlight the work of American psychologist Robert B. Cialdini. In his 2001 *Scientific American* article, "The Science of Persuasion," Cialdini detailed the six inclinations at play when we talk about persuasion. Cialdini spells out the things causing us to act. With most of these tendencies, I envision a flashing yellow light (proceed with caution) and for some, I see red (stop). My warning: There's a line between persuading and applying misleading/inappropriate pressure that can be tempting to cross when a customer just needs a final nudge. Here's how I see it, using Cialdini's six inclinations:

- **Reciprocation:** The expectation that a gift, good deed, or kind gesture be repaid.

Persuasion with integrity: A customer should never feel as if they owe you anything. You're fixing a problem, not setting them up for a future favor.

- **Consistency:** Messaging/word choices that promote a commitment.

  Persuasion with integrity: Consistency in messaging is a tenet of marketing, but the message should always be truthful—*always.* Telling the same lie over and over again is not the consistency that promotes a healthy relationship.

- **Social validation:** Peer pressure (others have already acted; so should you).

  Persuasion with integrity: Highlight another reputable person or organization that has already acted if it will legitimize your offer or ask. My word of caution: Due to privacy and confidentiality issues, many do not want their names mentioned in such a manner. Get permission before turning to social validation.

- **Liking:** Personal connection (it's easier to say no if they don't like you).

  Persuasion with integrity: Does the customer like you? This one is near and dear to my heart, as I have seen many a salesperson struggle with the concept that being likable matters. They might like themselves (as many of us salespeople do), but the customer does not share that same view. A surprising number think that good products and services alone are all they need, and being polite and friendly are a waste of a customer's precious time. I'll skip the Golden

Rule lecture and just say this: Make it your mission to be liked for all the right behaviors—you're polite, on time, clean, positive, a great (reflective) listener, and a person of integrity.

- **Authority:** Flexing your subject matter knowledge to lend credibility to your product, cause, or ask. *Persuasion with integrity:* If you have an academic-like respect for the facts, your claims of authority should never lead you astray. In other words, don't ever bullsh*t your customers (especially when it comes to what's verifiable).

- **Scarcity:** Limited supply of goods, services, time, etc. *Persuasion with integrity:* Alerting a customer to supply issues and time constraints is smart. Fabricating scarcity to create a false sense of urgency ("act now before it's too late") will eventually bite you.

In relationship sales, to use persuasion is to use facts (uncovered throughout discovery sessions) packaged in a way to influence the buyer to improve some aspect of their business (a need). There is nothing negative or deceptive about that scenario. On a personal level, I guarantee you can think back to a time when a purchase from a salesperson felt good hours, days, or even months later … something made your life easier, fixed a problem, or helped you feel more capable or attractive. You were OK with persuasion then! As for your customer, they might not feel better-looking after your sale, but the purchase should cure some woe (and definitely make them feel smarter). OK, with persuasion's good name cleared and our morality in check, let's get up off the therapy couch.

CLOSING THE INTERACTION

Let's bring this tango to a *resolución*, shall we? This is the moment we have been building toward (me too, honestly) ... the finale of your unique dance! You've built real rapport and truly understand your customer's needs; it's time to sweep them off their feet. Let's bring value to the dance floor via some powerful *persuasive* communication that delivers solutions and closes the interaction the PSC way, checking off our two final steps.

1. Build rapport
2. Understand needs
3. **Deliver solutions**
4. **Close the interaction**

The PSC Persuasive Process follows a basic yet effective three-part blueprint: an ***introduction*** with a stated purpose and pitch teaser; a ***body*** filled with facts, evidence, and your solution; and a ***conclusion*** where you review and go for the kill. As I stated earlier, think of this process as a package. This parcel delivers the entire story of the salesperson/customer journey you have been piloting, in a concise, action-prompting package. Your customers will appreciate the straightforward nature of this approach, guaranteed, and be ready to act at its conclusion. The following steps will lead you naturally (by being persuasive) to a sale. As always, here's an outline:

The Persuasive Formula:

a. **Introduction**
   - State the purpose
   - Confirm time frame
   - Confirm agenda and preview solution (pitch teaser)
   - Check in where appropriate

b. **Body**
   - Facts about the customer
   - Overview of the customer's needs
   - Evidence, facts, and strengths about your company
   - Your solution using benefit-centric language (your proposal)

c. **Conclusion**
   - Check in
   - Restate solution
   - Select an appropriate close
   - Make your ask
   - Remain silent

Does all of that sound familiar? It should. Remember the winning strategy for any speech we covered a few chapters back: (1) tell the audience what you are about to tell them **(introduction)**, (2) tell them **(body)**, then (3) tell them what you just told them **(conclusion)**. As you can see, we apply the same formula here (talk about demystifying sales!). Now, let's dig deeper into each part by using the story of that first six-figure sale I made. (The one with the VP riding shotgun, yup, that one!)

THE PERSUASIVE FORMULA: INTRODUCTION

STATE THE PURPOSE

I was in the tire-selling business. The commercial tire business, to be exact. Think *Smokey & The Bandit*, but bigger. I dealt with large regional and national trucking companies hauling everything from vegetables to the latest gadget ordered online. One particular trucking fleet was a major produce hauler in California's central valley. Attempting to depose a major competitor, I had scheduled a meeting as the culmination of six months of putting in the work. Tracking through my sales process, I had qualified the fleet as a worthwhile target, built rapport, found a need, and designed a solution. Now, it was time to make my pitch. My purpose was something like the following:

> *"Thank you for meeting with us today. Throughout the last six months, you've shared a lot of your time with me. I don't take that for granted, as I know your role is critical to the livelihood of this company. I've also sincerely appreciated the access you've afforded me. That access has allowed me to collect a great deal of performance data related to your tire needs. I have a presentation queued up to walk us through my findings, complete with figures that support an overall future cost savings of 17 percent on your annual tire budget."*

Simple, direct, and to the point. **In a nutshell, "I'm here to showcase evidence that equates to a real financial benefit, not just theory."** I've teased a 17-percent savings on a big spend item; there is not a customer alive who would not want to hear what I had to say. Large truck and trailer tires, by the way, are one of the top costs incurred by a commercial trucking fleet. I've also given some sincere thanks. Every salesperson takes precious time away from those we call on; say thank you to them.

CONFIRM TIME FRAME

This one is as simple as it sounds. I needed 15-20 minutes to get through my material and wanted to include time for questions. My confirmation sounded like this:

> *"My presentation should take 30 minutes or less. Are we still good with that timeframe?"*

Why is this important? Simple: You want to know if you still have the amount of time you prepared for. If you practiced giving a 30-minute presentation but the customer is short on time, it's best to know the constraints before you get started. Remember: Plan, but don't be married to the plan because you might need to pivot.

CONFIRM AGENDA/PREVIEW

At this point, you've stated your purpose and know your time constraints. Now, run through your agenda. Mine sounded like this:

"Here is a quick agenda for you. I plan to:

- *review a few facts about your company—I'd like to share what I have learned,*
- *highlight the needs that we agreed on,*
- *tell you about how my company's strengths and my own align with your company and its needs, and*
- *conclude with my cost-saving solution.*

Sound good?"

The casual "Sound good?" is one of my go-to persuasive check-ins. It's a natural way to ask for permission to keep rolling. Though such permission may not seem like part of persuasion at first blush, if we revisit the second rule of persuasion ("to influence, and influencing is the power of producing effects by invisible *action*"), it truly is. I just gave them the roadmap detailing where I wanted to take them, I teased my savings and findings, and then casually asked if I should keep going. This agenda is so tangible it could be printed and held in one's hand, but my use of the question "Sound good?" is *invisible*. The buyer will unconsciously respond in the affirmative, wanting me to proceed. Simple, powerful stuff!

CHECK IN WHERE APPROPRIATE

Pay attention to body language and audible cues throughout your time with your customer. Check in when you feel you've possibly lost them. A pause and a question like "Make sense?" is a quick way to check for understanding. Use simple check-in questions to keep your customers engaged and part of the show. Losing your audience to their unasked and unanswered questions is a tragic, unnecessary way to lose a sale.

THE PERSUASIVE FORMULA: BODY

Facts about the customer

In my experience, new and untrained salespeople rarely present facts about the customer to the customer, dismissing this meaningful step as unnecessary. That's a shame. When using the PSC Persuasive Process, we fully lean into the opportunity to briefly tell your customer that you "get them." I'm not talking about anything lengthy, just a handful of bullet points that showcases your understanding of their business: what they make, what they sell, their main suite of services, are they a public or private company, are they local, regional or national, any awards they have won and so on. When presenting these facts using a PowerPoint-type/ digital format, I've never devoted more than one slide to this step—it's the perfect amount of space and will keep you from going overboard. My facts about my customer sounded like this:

"I want to share a few things that I have learned about your company over the last six months:

- *Founded in 1981 by two brothers, the company started as a family business and remains one today.*
- *From a humble two-truck beginning, the fleet now boasts over 200 trucks, making you one of the largest trucking companies in California's Central Valley.*

- *Historically focusing much of its energy in the agricultural hauling space, the company recently branched out into the bulk hauling and dry van segments.*
- *The company operates three terminals, with this facility acting as your headquarters and main maintenance facility.*

Does that sound accurate?"

Saying that I'm a fan of this part of the process is a huge understatement. When I notice this step missing from my salespeople's proposals, I always coach each offender to spend a couple of minutes, literally just two minutes, talking about the customer. Untrained, we are quick to jump right into solutions, robbing ourselves of one more awesome chance to build rapport in this manner. And here you thought you were done with rapport? Nope, sorry, you're never done with it. You've built rapport all throughout your interactions, and now you're actually doing it inside of your pitch! And what about my "Does that sound accurate?" check-in? This should elicit a smile from your customer, as they will appreciate that you took the time to pause and acknowledge what makes them tick. It worked in my pitch to the trucking customer, and many more after it. Word of caution: Don't simply copy and paste from a website; using your own words will keep you clear of simply sounding like a parrot. Wow ... kind of sounds like reflecting, right?

OVERVIEW OF THE CUSTOMER'S NEEDS

When I look back on this customer's needs, I appreciate the simplicity: They needed a quality tire at a competitive price. Every year, they put their annual tire business out to bid to major manufacturers, securing every tire they would need for the upcoming year. This bulk-buying practice saved them money, time and stress. The approach also gave them ultimate negotiating power with multiple bidders. I stated my customer's needs like this:

> *"As we agreed, your need is a quality tire, which you wish to purchase in bulk to last the year for your truck-specific wheel positions (steer and drive). You are looking at Tier 1 manufacturers for an overall level of performance and a high residual value of the spent product (the tire casings) at the end of its original life. Am I on target?"*

The need I stated was nothing more than what we had agreed on during discovery sessions. I did not overcompli-cate or embellish the need. If you notice, I used the words "we agreed"—words that remind the customer that *we* had settled on this need before this meeting. If you've made it to a final proposal, the need you highlight should never be a shock to your audience. Never. If you have engaged in quality discovery sessions along the way, needs would have organically taken shape from those passing, almost offhand customer statements (after masterfully placed questions) that you then breathed life into with reflections and follow-up questions.

EVIDENCE, FACTS, AND COMPANY STRENGTHS

Though many new salespeople omit stating facts about the customer, few forget to (humbly) brag about their own company. Imagine that! Don't get me wrong; presenting evidence, facts, and company strengths has its place, and that place is right here—but a word of caution. Think of the ability to share what you learned about the customer as your ticket to talk about your own company. If you neglect to showcase what you know about *them*, you have not earned the right to brag about *you*.

Here's the catch: Anything you say about your company should relate directly to the need you are highlighting. I know you could share a whole slew of amazing things that make your company great, but if they do not relate to your audience's actual needs (even indirectly), you'll lose their attention. Promise. In our ongoing example, my evidence, facts, and strengths sounded like this:

> *"Next up, I want to highlight a few aspects about my company that relate directly to your need. First, we are a Tier 1 manufacturer. Known for our performance and quality, our tires are trusted the world over. Our workmanship and materials shine with a national warranty rate of less than 1 percent. Second, our casings have the highest resale value of any manufacturer. Dealers will pay more for one of our casings than anything else in the market. And third, one of our core values relates to a healthy respect for facts, which I plan to highlight in the delivery of my solution."*

Everything I mentioned is directly tied to my customer's needs (quality tire, Tier 1, casing value). I could've shared my company's other superior qualities: patenting the blueprint for the modern tire, pioneering airless tire technology, etc. As tempting as these were, no other facts related *directly* to my customer's needs. Moral of the story: Keep your eye on the prize. Remember, when you're being persuasive, you don't need anything that detracts from your message, even those qualities you're proud of.

PRESENTING YOUR SOLUTION USING BENEFIT-CENTRIC LANGUAGE (AND PUTTING IT ALL INTO DOLLARS)

The scenario I painted sounds easy enough: *Put forth a good, comparable product at the best price.* There is an easy button here, but most of us won't want to press it—we're missing data and facts. Those supporting details become more and more important the hotter the competition is related to your particular selling environment. If you're looking for a poor close rate (which I know you are not), simply offer up your product at a price that makes you comfortable without supporting data and facts. In relationship sales, to use persuasion is to use facts (gently kicking dead horse here). If you sell a premium product or service (like I did), I am confident that you have access to fact after fact supporting your claims, but do you use them? Do you showcase them in a way that utilizes benefit-centric language? That language sounds like, "If you purchase _____ because it does _____, you will get _____ benefit." In my world, that benefit is always in dollars. But what if something saves the customer time, you might ask? That time can always be converted into dollars saved. You see where I'm going with this one!

Let's lift the hood on my favorite auto manufacturer to illustrate a quick point regarding your price tag. You should present your product's or service's price tag as the combination of the positives and negatives related to ownership—the good minus the bad—over time. Your upfront price is one thing, but is there more to the story over time? Say you're selling used Land Rover Range Rovers. The lines, shape, elegance, and capabilities of this vehicle lineage are legendary. (I'm obsessed with them. I love them. I'd own a dozen if I could.) The downside is that depending on the year, they can become a maintenance money pit. That's why they're a great example of price vs. cost: You might pay _____ dollars for a Range Rover, **the price**, but the **true cost** from never-ending mechanical and electrical gremlins could end up being much higher. (I still love you, Land Rover. Sincerely.)

Moral of the story: Be certain you can prove what you're selling is worth the upfront price, and be ready to account for any shortcomings that can impact the true cost of your solution *before your customer brings them up*. In the same light, be proud of your high price—justify and defend your awesomeness with facts. If you can equate your solutions to dollars, do it, do it, do it. Talking in terms of revenue generation or savings is the gold standard when presenting solutions.

My solution sounded like this:

"When I stated my purpose, I mentioned bringing forth a tire solution that would save you 17 percent on your annual tire budget compared to what you are running today. We agreed that your need was a quality tire, which you wish to purchase in bulk to last the year for your truck-specific wheel positions (steer and drive).

"As you know, I have been tracking our test tire performance throughout this last year (a sample of tires I placed in the

*fleet to gain data). I have also been tracking the perfor-
mance of your current tires, my main competitor. As we
approached this day, I never hid the fact that I thought my
initial price point would be higher than any competitor
bidding for your business. The data collected was critical in
extrapolating true savings related to overall performance.*

*"Knowing that I would need to justify my higher price
points, I used my competition's bid-winning prices from last
year and applied some predictive logic to where I thought
their bid for this year might land. I took into consideration
the historical pricing gap between our two companies
and price increases seen in the industry over the last 12
months. With that information, along with performance
data, I could fully calculate a fleet consumption prediction
for next year using my tires and their tires, down to the
penny. The following brings this all together."*

Next, I presented my research on their consumption.
When selling a product with a performance lifespan, a
consumption model should be your go-to in proposing
solutions. Through some simple math, you can accurately
predict how many widgets a customer will consume in a
given time period. The more complete your data is, the
stronger your calculation can be. Then, if you know how
the customer uses the widgets (to make sure your compar-
isons will hold up) and how your widget performs versus
how the competition's widget performs, you can pinpoint
consumption numbers ... and from there, compare true
prices and costs for your customer.

"If running my steer tire, I calculate you would consume approximately 334 units next year. At the current performance levels of my competition, that equates to purchasing <u>166 fewer steer tires from us</u>.

"If running my drive tire, I calculate you would consume approximately 267 units next year. At the current performance levels of my competition, that equates to purchasing approximately <u>53 fewer drive tires from us</u>.

"Using my price points, I have calculated that the consumption of my product would cost you approximately $194,000. Continuing to run your current manufacturer of choice would cost you approximately $234,000. Your savings equates to 17 percent! Not to mention, you're changing 219 fewer tires."

Wow, that's powerful! Using benefit-centric language allowed me to communicate real savings in real dollars. To take that a step further, I could have even equated a dollar figure to the time it would save changing 219 fewer tires.

That was the culmination of a year spent building a relationship and rapport, placing test products, many days climbing around trucks and rummaging through vehicle files, asking the right questions, listening, and, most importantly, reflecting ... in the end, all packaged in persuasion.

Like this one, the vast majority of my sales were heavily driven by data. We joke about why we have to learn algebra, but I'm here to tell every high school student that I use it nearly every day. (Remember those word problems? 'One number is 3 times another number. If you add 17 to each, the first resulting number is twice the second resulting number. What are the two numbers?') Well, I chose to live in this world (me and my calculator, that is) to arrive at the best possible solution and presentation. I spared this customer and others the pain of showing all my work during the presentation (insert yawn here), but I left a copy of my supporting data. If a customer had watched me put the work in over weeks and months, rarely would they question my calculations. However, that copy of my data and figures was oh so important because almost everyone has someone who they answer to, and the last thing you want to do is leave them scrambling to defend their decision to say 'yes' to you. Rapport and trust flow back and forth between you and your customer. When they look smart, you look smart. No buyer's remorse here.

Although math related to widget performance was a huge part of my discovery and design processes, it might not carry the same weight in yours, depending on your business. (A heartfelt apology for any algebra nightmares this chapter awakened.) Regardless, and to reiterate, you should somehow be conveying a benefit over time. In the next chapter, we'll hear from business owners and leaders who use other skills that complement persuasion.

Let's bring this sales pitch home, shall we?

THE PERSUASIVE FORMULA: CONCLUSION

CHECK IN

It's time to check in with your customer, but this is not the time for "Make sense?" or "Sound good?" In this pivot to the conclusion, my check-in sounded like this:

"Any questions before I conclude?"

This prompt gives your customer one last chance to bring forth an objection or ask for clarification. At this point, I was always willing to discuss or defend my math. What I love about math (I'm a closet mathlete, if you can't tell) is that math has only right and wrong answers—you can't be half right or a little bit wrong. Before the meeting, I would've checked my calculations backwards and forwards to be ready for any questions. The tighter my story (with facts) tied directly to dollars (via math), the more likely I was to get an instant green light at my closing. If your customer does have questions or concerns, get ready to reflect, baby. Use your skills of reflection to answer their concerns fully.

RESTATE THE SOLUTION

It's time to walk through your story again, but in an abridged form, loosely using the model for that perfect speech. My restated solution sounded like this:

"Now, I'll summarize today's discussion. Your need is a quality tire, which you wish to purchase in bulk to last the year for your truck wheel positions. You are looking at Tier 1 manufacturers for an overall level of performance and the residual value of the spent product (casing) at the end of its original life. Not specifically called out when we started but through our interactions, you have stated that the overall value and performance of the product, if it could be shown, would trump acquisition price. I said I believed I could save you 17 percent on your tire budget and brought data to support that claim.

"My solution equated to a 17-percent cost savings, with a significant reduction in the number of tires needed. Running my product, I calculated that you would need 166 fewer steer tires this year and 53 fewer drive tires. That's significant! Using my price points, I calculated that the 17-percent cost savings using my product equated to savings of $40,000 next year."

And that, folks, was my mic drop, my "show me the money" moment! There's only one thing left to do after this: Close. The. Sale.

SELECT AN APPROPRIATE CLOSE

There are all kinds of closes: direct (ask for the order), assumptive ("You've had great luck with ____; how about we try _____ next?"), contingency ("We can start by servicing 30 today; after two months, how about we finish the other 30?"), alternative/forced choice ("Would you prefer we start picking up on Mondays or Wednesdays?"), the recommendation ("I recommend you take 50 today, and the remaining hundred in a month"), and impending event/ fear of loss ("This discount expires next month. If you go ahead now, you won't miss out").

Personally, my go-to is the direct close (and sometimes alternative/forced choice). The others are all fine and have their place but can tiptoe into sounding sales-y to me. If we've persuaded with facts, we can (and always should) skip sales-y. The direct close is just that—direct—nothing sales-y. It also matches the effort put forth in the PSC Persuasive Process. You've done your work and shown your worth, now you can ask for the order. Simple. With the alternative/

forced choice, you can ask the customer to pick between this or that solution, perfect for when you can present options. (Options make people feel more in control.)

Since I'm a direct-close fan and it fits here, we're going to make Brad Pitt's *Fight Club* character proud and simply ask for the order. In one of my favorite scenes from this David Fincher classic, Ed Norton's character hints at needing a place to stay (after his apartment blew up, that is); Pitt's character urges Norton's to stop beating around the bush and just make the ask. I love this scene for many reasons, but specifically for how it relates to closing a sale. I mentioned early that the customer would likely be rooting for you to make the sale if using all things PSC. So go for it! Ask.

Challenge accepted, Brad. I chose the direct close.

MAKE YOUR ASK

In this scenario, I made my ask as a statement:

> *"Let's save you $40,000 and reduce your annual tire consumption by over 200 tires."*

Wrap your mind around that approach: I asked a question without asking a question. This should look familiar; a direct close using a statement is similar to how a reflection is an inferred (invisible) question. I'm also not looking for a closed-ended "yes" or "no" answer. I'm looking for something a little bigger.

REMAIN SILENT

We've all heard the phrase, "The person who talks first loses." It's cliché but happens to hold some degree of truth in sales. Once we've officially made our ask, we should shut our traps. Continuing to talk after you've made your ask muddies your proposal and gets your customer's mind wandering. Sincerely, stop talking after your ask is made. If you're like me, you will grow to love the silence between your ask and the customer's next words. The anticipation produces a wonderful natural high.

So, what came next for me? I sure as hell would not write about a lost sale! He was in. His reflection-like "yes" sounded like this: "I appreciate the work you've put into this. Let's make it happen."

My wins got bigger over the years, but this one was special. The morning of this sale, that vice president asked me, "What are we going to do today?" I had looked him in the eye and said, "We're going to sell 500 tires." I'll never forget his cynical grin and non-confidence-boosting chuckle, which made the win that much sweeter! After the sale, I earned his sincere smile and words of approval.

In summary, be proud to use persuasion. If you employ the PSC lessons you've learned, you earn the right; I sincerely hope this chapter showcased that fact. Everything up to this point has been leading us to assembling this persuasion-wrapped package. Use this process; I promise it won't lead you astray.

A NOTE ON NEGOTIATION

Some of you might be wondering where the chapter is on negotiation—well, it's not in this book. The idea of PSC is centered around presenting a fact-based case requiring minimal, if any, negotiation. If you've followed the process, typically nothing is left to negotiate. It's a lack of facts and value presented that leaves us open to negotiation. A quick story to illustrate:

I once presented a PSC-style presentation to an owner and one of his managers. The format in this chapter was followed to the T. I detailed a fact-based cost savings and asked for the order. The manager spoke first and asked for a discount on my price. In the most polite way possible, I stated that my 'discount' was in the money that my product would save their company. The owner responded immediately. He asked his manager to stop (negotiating for the sake of negotiating) and accepted my proposal. PSC and math for the win! (My first six-figure sale is a forever memory, but this one tops my list of favorites, too.)

Negotiation is neither good nor bad. In many sales situations, we should all expect negotiations to take place. Never be surprised if a customer wants to negotiate with you. Even though PSC can help you guard from having to lower your price, there is always a chance that a customer will threaten to walk. My small word of negotiation advice: Be confident in the price you ask for, but know (ahead of time) how low you are willing to go in case you truly need to negotiate. You never want to be without that number in your pocket. In this example, I indeed had that number in my figurative pocket but never needed to reach for it. PSC might be just the thing that keeps that number safe in your pocket more times than not.

I'll close this chapter by briefly touching on solutions, setting up the next chapter. For the bulk of my career, I have sold tangible items, things you could touch, feel, and use.

Not everyone reading this book is selling something that can easily be quantified and equated to money. Your solution might be a service or an intangible like consulting, website design, or a marketing campaign. Your solution might be the opportunity for someone to do good (and feel good) if you're in the nonprofit world. Whatever your solution, it's your job to quantify what's in it for your customer. Any proposal lacking an answer to the age-old 'what's in it for me' (the customer) likely is doomed from the start.

In the next chapter, we'll hear from successful business leaders from various sectors about listening and value creation.

REFLECT

9

A Universal Truth
Listening is (almost) everything

Listening is (almost) everything. There, I said it, and I won't take it back. In this chapter, I want to affirm for you that *quality listening is everything (just about everything)*, regardless of what you sell. Period.

As I alluded to earlier, this universal truth can be applied to any human interaction. If I were to ask you for three qualities of your best friend, I can almost guarantee that one of them would be that they listen. When you are with this person, you feel heard. If we use our bucket analogy, they let you empty yours. It's as simple as that—every woman,

man, child, student, customer, employee, voter, etc., wants to be heard. It's the key to any healthy relationship, sales relationships included.

As you know by now, I mostly have sold physical objects that could be held, used, consumed, shipped, delivered, or installed. My pitch (related to an agreed-on need) typically involved **features** (specific pieces of technology), **advantages** (what the technology did/achieved), and **benefits** (the revenue generated or costs saved). In the last chapter, we walked through one of my all-time favorite pitches, a big win early in my career that still brings a smile to my face all these years later. I used a *total cost of ownership* model in the presentation with real numbers, showing the customer the impact my products would have on their bottom line over time. The moment the customer said "Let's make it happen," I solidified the largest single sale of my career and started a lifelong love affair with all things PSC. A total rush!

That was my world for the last 20+ years … What about yours? What do you sell (something I hope you have been thinking about the entire time you have been reading)? You might not sell objects. You might sell services, something creative, or even coaching or consulting. Does everything related to PSC equate to your world? I say an unequivocal yes, but know there are other things we need to highlight.

If listening is *almost* everything, what else matters in taking your sales to the next level? When is it OK to challenge the customer? How important is it to get the small things right and do great work? What about connections within your own organization? And what about your customer's (and our own) running parachutes (devices that expand and create drag the faster you go, forcing you to work harder and get stronger)?

To answer these questions, to fill the void left by a word like 'almost,' I enlisted the help of successful friends and mentors. Every one of them has sold something different. In their forthcoming words of wisdom, they all stress the importance of listening but take us in a few different directions. I could not be more excited to showcase their thoughts on communication as well as other golden nuggets of sales advice. Let's go!

KRISTA SKIDMORE
CEO/FOUNDER, FLASHPOINT LEADERSHIP CONSULTING

"The more we listen and learn, the more insight we gain, the greater the value we can show and provide to our client."

Krista Skidmore operates her business in the world of human resources and people development. FlashPoint has worked with such clients as the Bureau of Land Management, the Nevada Department of Transportation, and Nintendo (which instantly conjures memories of *Zelda* and my parent's basement). In an email discussion with me on March 21, 2023, she wrote:

> "We work with *Fortune* 1000-level C-Suite executives looking to build bench strength, retain talent, increase engagement, promote inclusion, and ultimately strengthen bottom-line results. Our services include leadership development programs, team effectiveness solutions, and coaching. I regularly frame

this message about our company: We don't do things *to* people; we do things *with* people.

"Especially in the consultative leadership development space, for me the sales process is all about deepening relationships … with time. Two-way communication or dialogue is crucial. We rarely enter a needs assessment conversation with a presentation or slide deck. How could we assume to know what they are experiencing until we have a conversation first? Rather, we listen, ask powerful questions, challenge where appropriate, share perspectives and insights, and then and only then do we recommend. With this process, our clients regularly share with us how they feel a part of the solution-building that takes place, and they feel as if they *own* that next step as their own plan. We call this co-creation.

"Sure, FlashPoint has something to bring to the conversation given our experiences, but the client has an equally important perspective to contribute to the dialogue. **The combination of *outsight,* us looking outward to learn from the client, and *insight,* the institutional knowledge a client brings to the table, is magical. In the end, it's not sales at all, but rather a collaborative answer to their specific need.** We find when we achieve this level of partnership that our impact and results are magnified, and we continue the relationship for years to come. And because we focus so much on making the client contact the hero of their story, it's not uncommon to see an open door at a new organization with a welcoming smile if they ever move on.

"When it comes to growth over the past 20 years, we have found the following connection to be true: The total number of individual relationships we have in a client organization correlates directly to the potential collective opportunity we have for more growth. In other words, we have worked hard to listen beyond just our original point of client contact. This represents a multiplicative effect for us. The more we listen and learn, the more insight we gain, the greater the value we can show and provide to our client. And when we do great work flawlessly, it begets more opportunities for impact within the same organization.

"I can't stress enough how our continuous communication and follow-through on commitments have shaped our growth and business longevity. Doing the small things as well as we do the big things has been our great equalizer, especially when our boutique brand competes regularly with big-box consultancies. It helps us punch above our weight class. As a leadership development firm, we must model what great leadership looks like every single day. That is partly about our integrity but also about our continuous learning mindset. We must keep growing—learning, unlearning, and relearning to meet a new context of leadership challenges and see around corners in the future."

Wow! So many of Krista's thoughts align with PSC. I love that she mentioned the use of "powerful questions." Powerful questions sound BIG to me, and they are! They're provocative but appropriate. They're smart, rooted in knowledge gleaned from past experiences, but never presumptuous. And the listening, reflecting, and challenging that takes place when a customer speaks—that's when the real co-creation or selling happens. We have spent a great deal of time talking about reflecting the customer's thoughts, ideas, and emotions but not a lot of time on the "challenging" that comes after, so I'm glad Krista mentioned it. **In the simplest terms, the right to challenge the customer, the idea that you might professionally and appropriately push back on something they say or do, is earned. It's only after they feel heard that this is appropriate.** When they feel heard and trust you, your challenge will feel natural and be welcome.

As Krista's model for success illustrates, the journey toward a solution becomes a shared one as relationships deepen. She describes a relationship in which the customer feels total ownership in the proposed solution and what comes next. She calls it co-creation, and I'm not sure there's a better way to describe what's happening here. Bravo!

Krista also keys in on the fact that both parties, the seller and customer, bring equally important contributions to the discovery table. Going back to my analogy of UPS and FedEx (Chapter 2), it's not a stretch to think that if a seller knew everything about FedEx's problems, they would have some insight into the potential woes at UPS—but where this goes off the rails is when the seller assumes that a *like* customer, seemingly similar in every way to an established one, could not possibly have anything new for us to tackle. Choosing not to make assumptions allows Krista's magic to happen, and the shared, authentic journey never feels like sales.

Two final nuggets from Krista are closely related: the multiplication factor and doing great work.

Doing great work sounds like a given, but I've seen many companies do subpar work, and rarely does that beget more opportunities. News of subpar work performance can travel like wildfire and kill the relationship (and prevent others). If you sell something that must be installed, like I have, not only does your product have to be good, but the service to install it has to be equally good. If the customer hates the installation experience of your wonderful product, you're sunk; they don't much distinguish between the two. If your core business is service, then your reputation is everything. On the flip side, if you do great work and have multiple contacts within an organization, positive news of your greatness can spread just as easily. Part of Krista's business is training—there's an aspect of service there. A number of years ago, I had the pleasure of attending one of FlashPoint's sessions of *The Leadership Challenge*® (training based on the book of the same name by Jim Kouzes and Barry Posner). Their execution was flawless, and you better believe I told everyone!

Connected at the hip to doing great work is the multiplication factor. I wish that I had understood this principle when I was younger in my career; I stuck to my main client contacts, unknowingly limiting my exposure. Don't make my mistake! What Krista describes can happen only when a wide variety of people know you and what you're bringing to the table.

Worth a look and closely related to this multiplication factor is the concept of *stakeholder mapping*, detailed by Professor John M. Bryson in his book, *Strategic Planning for Public and Nonprofit Organizations, 5th Edition (2018)*. This mapping concept is about knowing your audience or cast of characters and the ways they can help you move an initiative or agenda forward (or hold it back). Related to the influence, or power, that different parties can have on your success, the act of stakeholder mapping, sometimes referred to as *power mapping*, puts individuals into buckets (not like Scott's bucket, by the way). These buckets help guide us in sharing information and the degree of involvement we should seek from different customer parties … In the simplest terms, who should be heavily involved (think of Krista's co-creation), who should be managed closely (because they could make or break our efforts), who should simply be informed, and who requires minimum attention. Why is this important? It sucks to spend your precious time with the wrong people only to be blindsided by an individual not even on your radar. When looking to penetrate deeper into an organization, map that cast of characters. You won't be sorry.

Regardless of where you are in your career, take Krista's advice and learn from my early missteps. Branch out within your customers' companies. Be seen, be known, and do great work.

Krista – thank you, friend.

TOM METCALF, FOUNDER OF TELENOTES (NOW VOZE)

"Companies can gain tremendous peace of mind if they strive to create a customer experience anchored in their own seamless, customer-centered internal communication."

Next, we will hear from Tom Metcalf, founder of **Telenotes** (now **Voze**), a customer relationship management (CRM) tool that outside salespeople (including me) love to use.* Started in 2000, Tom's Utah-based company made its mark by being an early disruptor in the world of computer-based CRMs. Telenotes, as you might have guessed, was a CRM that used voice dictation to record sales calls; customer interactions could be recorded quickly on the fly, sans keyboard, simply by leaving a voicemail. Voze, the evolution of Tom's original CRM company, has continued to shake things up as an early adopter of AI and machine learning while keeping true to its voice-driven roots. In an email on January 15, 2024, Tom wrote:

> "It's always been about the salesperson for us. At Voze, we work with companies who employ field-based sales teams to grow their businesses. We pride ourselves in putting the salesperson first, providing them with a tool they see value in using; the companies who use Voze also put their salespeople first. The result of our focus is not only that the field-based salesperson values our service, but also that the associated C-suites and managers love the relevant, detailed, and timely information they can gather from their teams using the platform. Additionally, a bonus to the service we provide is that for the first time in many sales

organizations, the inside support team or home office now has real-time information they've only dreamed about in the past. Too many CRM's are black holes of information where customer details are keyed in and forgotten. And a black-hole CRM is the furthest thing I can think of from great communication. This is not the case with Voze.

"As it relates to communication, there is an interesting dynamic at play for the field sales representative. On one hand, the anonymity and freedom that comes from being 'outside' is liberating and very desirable for most salespeople. They are the faces of the companies they represent and often have the final word in making the sale. Sometimes, they might even appear mysterious. But that same anonymity has its drawbacks. One can be the lack of connectedness and communication that is inherent for those who collaborate in an office setting every day. While external communication with customers is vital to the success of any company selling their goods and services, the type of connectedness and communication I'm referring to is what's found within an organization: inside support teams to outside field-based salespeople … sales *managers* to sales *people*.

"What is all too common in organizations of any size is a lack of connection between inside and outside teams. The deal of the century could be cemented by a salesperson, only to quickly fall apart without the proper communication and coordination between all the individuals needed to pull it off. The recipe for success, to use a sports analogy, is that every player on the team needs to be 'mic'd up;' everyone needs to be on the field and sideline, working as a team. A lack of communication looks like something else: players on the field, coaches in the locker room, physical therapists and trainers on the bus. Sounds nuts, right? Pro sports teams don't operate like this, but I'm sorry to say that many corporations do, siloing communication that should be shared for the good of achieving common goals.

"Companies can gain tremendous peace of mind if they strive to create a customer experience anchored in their own seamless, customer-centered internal communication. Two different personal experiences come to mind when thinking about this concept. The first relates to calling my preferred airline. I fly a lot, so this experience is near and dear to my heart. When I call said airline, they address me by my name, have my schedule at their fingertips, and know my aisle-versus-window preference. How cool is that? I feel like they really know me. And it doesn't matter who answers the phone; the experience is the same every single time, and since not every phone call is of a positive nature (things happen to us travelers), that feeling of being known becomes even more important. It's this feeling of connection that keeps me coming back again and again.

"My second experience conjures feelings of being a number, the exact opposite of calling my preferred airline. I recently took my snowblower to a shop for repair. They called me later and left a voice message with the amount it would cost to complete the service and asked me to call with my approval. In response, I too left a voice message in which I approved the repairs. A few days later, my inner voice was urging me to call back just to make sure they had gotten the message. Turns out, they had not received my message, or at least did not acknowledge receiving it, nor did they appear to have any sort of follow-up protocol in place. In this instance, a lack of internal communication on their part resulted in a delay in getting my machine back to me, as well as them not turning a job quicker for revenue purposes. This experience by no means crushed my faith in humanity, but I sure as heck did not feel as if they knew me.

"The airline experience is what we should all be striving for with our customers. How wonderful would it be for a customer to call your office/branch/warehouse and speak with an inside salesperson with easy access to the discussions you and the customer had recently? There would be less frustration on both sides when it came to quoting prices, discussing new products, or any other important details that might come up. The best-case scenario: You are so in sync with your inside team that they never need to speak with you before acting. Beautiful, seamless, customer-centered communication.

"In your role, you might be the tip of the spear in the field, but don't forget about the army of people supporting you in the background. Your communication with those individuals can make the difference between your company being seen as the attentive airline or the uncaring repair shop. Salespeople who use Voze in the field instantly inform their inside counterparts or sales managers of details and situations that will help move the needle when it comes to sales. **Seamless communication within a sales organization is directly reflected in customer satisfaction today and more business from that customer and others in the future.**

"And if you're dying to know, my preference is a window seat."

Just like Krista, Tom hit on something that needs more attention—great internal communication. His words remind us that sales is not a solo gig. My most prosperous times as a salesperson, some predating the use of advanced CRMs, all had one thing in common: I was in a type of symbiotic relationship with my inside counterparts. We talked constantly, and consistently pulled in the same direction. I don't think I fully understood the significance of these special relationships at the time, but I do now.

I have been fortunate enough to use several CRMs throughout my career, seeing their transformations firsthand from the driver's seat. My time behind the CRM steering wheel included years using one of the most recognizable CRMs in the world, where I was a "key user" (fancy title for someone who could teach others how to use it). My biggest takeaway: Value creation and attitude have everything to do with a CRM's worth, and they are directly related ... something Tom has always understood. Let me explain.

If salespeople are asked to key in information about their customers and prospects but know it'll never be used for anything worthwhile (Tom's black hole), then they will see little value in the task of inputting those details. On the other hand, if that same information is used by everyone on the team to generate revenue and strengthen relationships, then the experience will be seen as one of magical sales enablement and attitudes (and follow-through) will be positive.

If you use a CRM, I challenge you to step back and look at how you use it, either as a salesperson or a sales leader. As a salesperson, if you choose not to interact with your teammates using the tool, you are missing out on an amazing opportunity to get everyone mic'd up and in the game with you. If you are disconnected from your support team, a customer reaching out to your company might feel like they just called Tom's repair shop, which sounds dreadful. If used as intended, CRMs like Voze can help organizations create Tom's sales utopia of "seamless, customer-centered communication." As a sales leader, if you are strictly counting calls per day and measuring a salesperson's pipeline, you too have missed a very important opportunity—the chance to coach and be present in the arena with your team members. Tom's analogy could not be more spot on! Professional sports head coaches are always in the mix, constantly communicating with their players and coaches on and off the field.

CRMs, once thought of as merely a digital contact book, have evolved to enable great communication at every level of an organization. Too many companies purchase CRMs that have sportscar-like features, but then decide to use it only for delivering pizzas. Crazy, right? If you purchased the sportscar, get the team to pile in (I know, they won't all fit, but you get it), start pushing some buttons, and mash on the accelerator. See what the thing can do!

For those of you not using a CRM, all of this still applies (and perhaps even more so!). The main question you need to answer is this: Do you have a system in place to ensure Tom's airline-like experience for your customers? The more complex a sale becomes, the more that the coordination phase in your sales process, where internal communication can really shine, becomes paramount. Gathering your team together to review the deal you just struck and talk through the contributions you expect from all involved will be key to your success. Tom's words are a great reminder that making the sale is one thing, but how we communicate as a team on the back end is everything.

Tom – thank you, friend.

STÉPHANE AND SHALEE SCHAFEITEL, AUTHORS OF *MASTER YOUR MINDPOWER*

> *"Focused listening is vital as we guide our clients to uncover their mental and emotional barriers—what we term 'running parachutes.'"*

Next, we will hear from Stéphane and Shalee Schafeitel (also known as Stéph and Shay), who are world-renowned Mindpower Coaches, authors, and speakers. Stéph and Shay are the authors of the *Wall Street Journal* bestselling-book *Master Your Mindpower: A User Manual for Your Mind & the Ultimate Guide to Mental Toughness*. Apple News recently featured them as the World's #1 Resilience Coaches. They help business leaders and high performers increase their mental toughness and emotional resilience; their work has already positively impacted the lives of millions of people. On a side note, Stéph and I shared a first employer and have been friends ever since. In an email dated March 10, 2024, Stéph and Shay wrote:

> "We have a saying in the coaching industry, borrowed from the Greek Stoic philosopher Epictetus: 'We have two ears and one mouth so that we can listen twice as much as we speak.' When coaching people to break through to greatness or reach that next level of success (whatever that may look like for them), it's critical to listen—and to listen well. Most of our time in coaching sessions is spent listening to our clients. We also have three specific stages at which we ask open-ended questions.

> "In our initial consultation, our goal is to gain clarity on their current needs and struggles so we can demonstrate how Mindpower Coaching can provide the solution they're looking for. We ask:

> 1. What's the biggest goal you must achieve this year?

2. What's the biggest problem in your life that if it were solved would have the biggest impact?
3. What's the cost of not solving this problem?
4. What will you gain when you solve this problem?
5. What will change in your Life? Business? Health? Relationships?

"This process helps clients clarify their needs and provides us with the necessary information to effectively communicate our value proposition. This clarity and understanding would be impossible to achieve without truly listening—to every single word our clients say, the unspoken words laden with meaning, and even the tone of their voice, which sometimes reveals more than the words themselves.

"A second instance where deep listening occurs is in our first coaching session, where we work closely with clients to define the outcomes they want to achieve. Our aim is not only to help them attain those outcomes but also to guide them to the mental clarity they seek. This step often results in a significant breakthrough, marking the start of a transformative journey. We ask such questions as:

1. What specifically do you want as an outcome from working together?
2. On a scale of 1 to 10, where are you now regarding this desired outcome?
3. On a scale of 1 to 10, where do you want to be regarding this desired outcome?
4. How will you know when this outcome is achieved?

5. What will you see/hear/feel/think when this outcome is achieved?

"Most of the time, clients aren't fully aware of what they want. Therefore, our ability to ask thought-provoking questions, truly listen to their responses, and assist them in gaining clarity is integral. This process not only sets the direction for our coaching relationship but also ensures that we're aligned with their ultimate goals. As author and speaker Stephen Covey aptly put it, 'Begin with the end in mind.' (*7 Habits of Highly Effective People*)

"Finally, and most importantly, focused listening is vital as we guide our clients to uncover their mental and emotional barriers—what we term 'running parachutes.' For those unfamiliar, a running parachute is a training device that athletes use to create additional resistance; when removed, it instantly leaves the athlete noticeably better, faster, and stronger. Throughout life, we all accumulate running parachutes that hold us back from living our best lives: anger, sadness, fear, guilt, and limiting beliefs—self-doubt, feeling not good enough, unworthy, insignificant, or the belief that one can't achieve financial freedom. We tend to collect these running parachutes from our experiences and the people we choose to associate with. Releasing our mental and emotional running parachutes allows us to immediately become better, faster, and stronger than ever before—just like those athletes on game day or race day. So, we ask our clients questions like these:

1. How do you know you have this problem?
2. How is the problem a problem for you?
3. When do you do it?
4. When do you not do it?
5. How long have you had/done this problem?
6. How will you know when this problem has disappeared?

"It is an absolute must to listen very carefully to every single word our clients use in this session and to pick up on every tonality shift. We write down everything our clients say, literally word for word. Missing one word could mean missing a whole running parachute, which could be detrimental to a client's success. If we help clients successfully discover and release their parachutes, they can dramatically enhance their personal and professional performance. That is why listening is paramount, especially in this session.

"The secret to making a massive impact as a coach lies not in what one says, but in what one hears. It's the great differentiator between the novice coach and the elite coach. This is why we tell our students, 'You need to have rabbit ears and not an alligator mouth.'"

There is so much goodness to unpack here! Notice any connection between sales and the questions Stéph and Shay ask their Mindpower Coaching clients? I hope your answer is an immediate yes! It's **discovery** on a personal level. They ask clients to answer key questions that can and will lead to a mental breakthrough. They ask clients what they want/ expect from the relationship, how they define success ('Big Effing Goals,' as they like to say), and dig deep to find the things holding individuals back from achievements. As a PSC sales professional, you are actually doing those exact same things for your customers. Mind blown!

I have had the pleasure of personally being coached by Stéph over the years. He has helped me through moments when I have felt professionally stuck, lost, and confused. I have answered all the questions listed above many times, each time leading to personal growth and clarity, but I didn't make the connection to business until now. Just like Stéph and Shay work toward helping individuals tap into their own potential, you endeavor to unlock something holding your customer back from greater success.

If you noticed, I mentioned being coached "over the years" and that I answered those same questions "many times." As in coaching, if we salespeople are doing it right, we will be with our customers for multiple breakthroughs. Stéph and Shay have many coaching relationships that span years of connection, helping business leaders and high performers break through mental barriers again and again. Relationship sales is no different, and by applying the PSC lessons you've learned and a few plays from Stéph and Shay, you could be working with any of your customers for years and years. #goals

One of the strongest correlations I see between PSC and Stéph and Shay's work, besides the tremendous emphasis on listening and understanding, has got to be the running parachutes concept. Just as we all personally have these unconscious drag devices slowing our own success and growth, so do our customers and the companies we interact with. Your customers' parachutes look like fears and past failures, set ways of thinking ('we've always done it this way'), and an individual's own head trash, all holding them back from seeing and achieving greater revenue, bigger savings, or inventing the next big thing to help our planet. These parachutes are alive and well in business, and it's our job to help customers learn how to lose them! And if you're thinking that reflecting plays a part here, you would be correct. As we ask questions, we know the answers are not always on the surface—we have to reflect.

I love what Stéph and Shay's work does for individuals looking to better themselves. My hope is that you see the correlations between their work and the idea that you, too, are a coach for your customers.

Stéph and Shay - thank you, friends.

So listening *is* (almost) everything ...

> There's also a time (once earned) to challenge the customer.

> We realize that getting the small things right and doing great work matters.

> Connecting the dots within your own organization is pivotal to your success.

> Elite, frequent-flier-like customer experiences will pay dividends.

Helping your customers cut their running parachutes should be a "Big Effing Goal."

Read on for a few parting words from yours truly.

10

Parting words
A love letter or two

I've experienced some amazing technological advances throughout my career. At the risk of dating myself, I hit the real world in email's infancy, when writing one was like crafting a letter. I saw paper contracts and fax machines give way to electronic documents and integrated ERP systems. I experienced the rise of apps and texting. And I had a front-row seat for the birth and explosion of e-commerce. Since hitting the professional scene in Y2K, saying that I've *seen* some things would be an understatement. I know some of you have, too.

These and a multitude of advances changed selling—or did they? I have adopted the latest sales processes many times only to realize they were largely the same as those already existing. I've created business plans, key account plans, and quarterly business reviews using the latest templates only to spot the commonalities between the formats. And I've used the latest CRM app that promised to supercharge my sales funnel only to be crushed by the weight of the busywork it created for me. Notice a theme?

The truth (looking at you, sales professionals and sales leaders) regarding the hottest new whatever: All the apps, templates, and processes out there share something in common with diet and exercise. Wait, what? Yup, they sure do: If you use them, they all work. Period. Has the Atkins diet resulted in weight loss for its subscribers? Sure has. Will a ketogenic diet produce similar effects? Affirmative. Is the Mediterranean diet known the world over as one of the most heart-healthy diets and a proven ticket to weight loss when placed against a traditional Western diet? 100-percent yes. Are all those new sales-related apps, templates, and processes promising increased sales and productivity any different? Nope. They all work. Trust me. Like diets, they all work—*if you work them.*

A HUMAN INVESTMENT

Why then do so many companies get excited about the next big thing in sales processes, planning, and apps? Three general reasons, in my view:

> **One, they have never used anything formalized:** no process, plan, or tool—they've been wingin' it, if you

will. They trust they have hired good people who are out there making it happen. These companies employ the true hustlers (that's a compliment, by the way). Often, these companies exist in a more competitive sales environment (think relationship sales with compensation skewed towards eat-what-you-kill). The no-process organization could also be a start-up with passionate individuals simply grinding it out, telling their story to anyone who will listen. Regardless of which shoe fits, at some point these companies will have an aha moment when they realize what got them *here* won't get them *there*, prompting someone to proclaim, "We need a sales process!" This is 100-percent logical, Matt Detjen-approved, in fact.

Two, companies simply stop using whatever they had been using, which is the norm. When and why do companies forget about sales processes and planning? Take this one to the bank: It's when business is rockin'! When numbers are good at any medium to large company, salespeople and sales leadership likely cannot describe the phases of their own sales process and do not question it much. Unfortunately, what goes up will eventually come down; not too many companies never see sales decline, and when numbers tank, that's typically when they are ready for a new process. Newsflash: The old one worked just fine; you likely just stopped applying it. Managers stopped using the process to coach and salespeople to guide their actions. If we go back to my diet analogy, the same rules apply: You made incredible strides with dialed-in nutrition and exercise, then, like many of us, you got comfortable and thought you could manage things on your own. Without the discipline of your plan, however, you start to slip and lose the progress you made. For businesses, add in a down economy and a host of negative variables, and leadership will be screaming that the process is always the problem. They are wrong.

Three, they lack (sales) heart. The key lessons taught in PSC (building real rapport, reflecting, and being persuasive) are largely missing from the company's sales culture. What got them *here* (with minimal investment in people or soft skills) won't get them *there* (a winning team with a ton of customer-centric *sales heart*). Rounding out my diet and exercise theme, these companies are often looking for that miracle drug or pill (a new _____ for a quick fix), when it's an investment in strengthening the minds and hearts of their sales team that is truly needed.

My love letter to all companies who sell something (and what company doesn't?):

Dear Company:

Find a process you like, use it, and don't walk away from it. If you do stray for whatever reason, just go back to the one you had. Remember, there is *likely* nothing wrong with your sales process. Never spend a boatload of money changing your discovery phase to your needs assessment phase, or vice versa. Please, I beg you.

If the economy turns cold and your numbers suffer, go back to basics. There is a good chance you still know how to win!

If your people lack communication skills and heart, invest in the training they need. Get them my book (shameless plug noted), a sales coach, or other vetted training. Sales will (likely) always be done by humans—invest in the things that will make them better (sales) humans.

Sincerely,

Matt Detjen

CREATE YOUR OWN COLLECTION OF METHODS

I worked for a company who asked me to write a sales process, as we had reached our "what got us here won't get us there" moment. It was an exciting challenge and, looking back, I could not be happier having had the experience. This was a huge aha moment for me, *the* moment when I spotted the commonalities between every process I had ever seen or been taught. It was the equivalent of realizing that your parental figures were every mythological saint and fairy growing up—Santa, Tooth Fairy, Easter Bunny … all the same person.

Listen, I've poked a little fun at the commonalities in sales processes, and I've probably been a bit harsh. The ever-so-common sales process is a must, seriously. What gets me is that most companies confuse one process (a singular roadmap) with a greater methodology (multiple methods, processes, and soft skills). **Next-level salespeople combine processes and multiple methods for greater success. The lessons of PSC represent a sales methodology, a collection of methods ... that *heart* we've been discussing.** I've often heard that you can't teach "heart," but I disagree. You can teach heart to those with an open mind.

My love letter to you, the salesperson:

Dear You:

As a salesperson, take every opportunity to work on your methodology—your collective craft. If you're offered public speaking or communication training, take it. If you're offered a sales coach, gladly accept. If you typically read fiction, feather in some time-tested nonfiction to sharpen your mind. If you can find a sales superstar to emulate, get to modeling!

Invest in you. The worst thing you can say to yourself is, "I've been doing this for years. I don't need any help." You consciously made a deposit into your own sales methodology bank account by reading this book—congratulations! It is my hope that this book inspires you to listen on a deeper level, reflect more, and always persuade with the facts. But don't stop here! Keep learning and growing. Your sales record will only get better.

Remember: The magic does not come from simply following a process. The magic comes from what you do within the process. From this day forward, I hope you sprinkle PSC into everything (sales) that you do.

Sincerely,

Matt Detjen

BE A LEARNER, ALWAYS

I have been fortunate; nearly every one of my employers has invested in my development by paying for ongoing training, like the one who paid for PSC all those years ago. At the opening of my PSC session, Jane's master facilitator, Vito Giordano, asked this question:

"Are you here to **learn**, are you here on **vacation**, or are you a **hostage?**"

To learn is obvious—the learner is happy to be there and legitimately wants to grow. The vacationer, on the other hand, is the individual just happy to be away from work for a few days, where learning something is incidental (and a great location is a bonus). And the hostage … well, they're present against their will. I was always a learner, even if I occasionally grumbled about the course's location (just keeping it real, folks). Especially as a willing participant in PSC training, I loved watching the vacationers and hostages come around and buy into PSC's good content. Since becoming a trainer, I can unequivocally say that turning vacationers and hostages into believers is incredibly rewarding. My advice: Make it a goal to be a learner from the start and always remain a learner. There are nuggets of knowledge in any reputable firm's training offerings, I promise.

To bring this back to where it all started: Jane's take on reflective/active listening and persuasion changed my life. I am forever blessed by her desire to strengthen the communication skills of all who had the privilege of taking PSC. My human interactions are forever stronger, my emphasis on understanding others forever greater, and my spark for persuasive selling forever lit. I hope at least a few of the nuggets on these pages have resonated with you. Challenge yourself to be a keener listener out there.

Good selling, friends!

No monies, goods or services were exchanged for including quotes, companies or products in this book. Just the author's gratitude.

REFLECT

Bio

Matt Detjen has led sales training for multiple companies, including one of the world's most recognizable brands. Over his 25+ year career, he has been an accomplished sales director, award-winning salesman, and trusted brand spokesperson. His debut business book, *REFLECT: The Art of Powerful Sales Communication*, was published in 2024.

Although Matt did not take a direct route to the training stage and classroom, it's no surprise he eventually found a home there. Studying to be an educator, he had hopes of shaping young minds post-bachelor's degree, but the pull of nonprofit causes proved too strong for him to initially resist. Before landing in the for-profit world, he would spend time on staff at an international collegiate social organization, a children's hospital fundraising arm, and a college annual fund department. Matt attributes much of his soft skill development to these early nonprofit experiences.

He would also chase his acting dreams throughout his career, securing several principal commercial roles while living and working in the Midwest. Besides being fun, his on-camera work taught him the finer points of storytelling, connection, and preparation.

Matt has seen sales from virtually every angle. He has sold, managed, and led training for two global manufacturers, successfully navigated reorganizations and restructures at a headquarters level, and even worked for two of his former customers. You will be hard-pressed to find a trainer and speaker more adept and adaptable than Matt.

After years of sales success, Matt now has the pleasure of shaping minds, young and old, on the importance of great communication. A Missouri native, he and his family now call South Carolina home. Matt brings experience, laughter, and connection to any size classroom or stage.

Made in the USA
Columbia, SC
26 September 2024

43103631R00085